D1549404

Thought
FOR
Food

TELEGRAPH
SUNDAY MAGAZINE

Thought
FOR
Food
My Family & Other Recipes
Denis Curtis

Published by the Sunday Telegraph,
135 Fleet Street, London EC4P 4BL

First published November 1982
© Sunday Telegraph and Denis Curtis 1982

Design by Martin Bronkhorst
Edited by Michael Doggart
Illustrations by James Marsh and Royston Edwardes

Printed in Great Britain by
Redwood Burn Limited, Trowbridge, Wiltshire.

ISBN 0 901684 82 1

CONTENTS

All recipes are for six people unless
otherwise indicated

*For Mother — without whom
none of this would have been possible
and to John Anstey who gave
me the chance*

My Family and Other Recipes

This book had its beginnings with a 2nd World War dried egg omelette. I had the reputation at the age of ten of being something of an expert at passing-off the yellow powder as a creditable substitute for the real thing. But substitute it was. My critical faculties, even at that tender age, would not allow me to present the counterfeit as genuine.

Let me now confess something which I have only previously told to my cousin Gerald. My subterfuge was helped because I used to fold into the dried egg mixture an egg white from a real egg. I was able to keep this secret from the rest of the family because of the sneaky way I came by my egg supply. I saved all the surplus vegetables from the table including several cabbages which had not yet been relegated to the waste bin. This vegetable waste I sold to Mrs Jones who lived up the hill surrounded by chickens and pigs. In return, Mrs Jones gave me sixpence, plus half-a-dozen fresh eggs as an occasional bonus. 'Well, it is not often', she would say, 'that I get such lovely quality produce. All fresh and none of it has to be picked over.'

I had to do something to gain a culinary reputation. I was surrounded by cooks, Mother idiosyncratically, being the best of the lot. She perfected the sauce Pizzaiola in a hotel bedroom in Milan between acts of *La Bohème* at La Scala, singing all the while. (Puccini meant it was going well, Verdi made me tremble and Wagner drove me under the table.) Then there was Grandmama, the traditionalist, who had a strong influence on my style. It is her recipe for Christmas pudding that appears on these pages. Readers tell me they have never tasted better; the secret with the pudding is its use of butter instead of suet. There was Aunt Maggie who taught me how to make puff pastry; Mrs Morgan from next door who made bakestone bread and showed me how to make 'pics' (Welsh cakes); among many others, Mrs Bevan, who made nettle pop which exploded with a loud bang as regular as clockwork every Sunday morning just as the chapel organ struck the opening chords of *Guide me oh thou Great Jehovah*; in the Cotswolds, there was Aggie who despised game, 'It is a sin of the flesh', she would droggel, 'along with punting, hunting, cigarette cards, and roses.' Now she is dead but not before she was reconciled to the cooking of pheasants, and not before she sent me her last recipe. 'I cannot say how it tastes', she said, 'for never a drop of alcohol has passed my lips.'

Meanwhile, I have learned many sophisticated tastes from travelling the world and adding an international 'family' of friends and their recipes to my collection: New York, Paris, London, Rome . . . to the list can be added ad-infinitum Lebanon, Malta, Israel, Belgium, Denmark, Holland, Sweden, Germany, Spain, the Mauritius . . . In Britain I began writing about cooking in Nova Magazine pushed along by that lovely agony aunt Irma Kurtz and nudged by other friends who had eaten my food. Molly Parkin: 'You owe it to the valleys, love'; Fenella Fielding: 'There is something so sexy about the way you cook'; and editor Priscilla Chapman: 'Unusually for a

8

cookery writer your recipes work.'
Restaurateurs have had their say too, from
the unpredictable Peter Langan to that
manipulator of the pots and pans in
Britain's only Michelin three star
restaurant, Albert Roux of Le Gavroche,
also taking in the cozy John Tovey of the
famous lakeland Miller Howe and that
remarkable restaurateur Robert Carrier.

But mainly the stories are of friends who
have come to eat at my house. The witty
American author: 'My God, if that's a light
lunch what'll dinner be like – Moby Dick
on toast'. Of Ken and Marie who turned up
on the wrong weekend but were left
blissfully unaware of their gaffe. Of writer
Lynn Barber who arrived at lunchtime to
interview me and who was so bowled over
with the dish I created for her that we
talked through to next morning. Of the
wayward Charles Osborne and friend Ken
who were so uncertain of their arrival time
that they forced me to devise yet another
'instant' dish to cope with their vagaries.
And of my assistants, particularly Paul
Christian Thomas Hulme for whom I
invented one of my favourite dishes as
reward for his meticulous attention to detail
— *Chicken Christian*.

The readers of course take star billing:
they are part of the 'family' that makes my
Thought for Food column a success. They
may not all appear in this edition — there's
not room. But my thanks are due to them
and the countless others who have yet to
make their entry into 'My Family and
Other Recipes'.

SOUPS

Strawberry and Cucumber Soup

Grandmama taught me The Ways of the World and in particular The Art of the Picnic. While eating she reminisced about the old days and told me of 'the virility of that Nijinsky'. I thought 'virility' a balletic term like *entrechat*, which confusion got me into much trouble in the gallery later. But punctuating the reminiscences were some superb and unusual dishes and on a hot summer's day one of my favourites was a strawberry and cucumber salad. It was arranged as prettily as a Victorian posy, seasoned and chilled and just before serving doused with dry champagne — for which I now substitute wine vinegar. I took this dish as my inspiration and concocted an unusual soup.

2 oz butter
1 cucumber peeled and sliced
½ pt milk
1 onion sliced
Handful of parsley
6 peppercorns
8 oz strawberries
½ pt double cream

Heat butter in a pan and in it sauté peeled and sliced cucumber for 10 minutes. □ Meanwhile simmer in milk onion, parsley and peppercorns. □ Strain milk over the cucumber and liquidise. □ Add seasoning. □ Liquidise strawberries and fold into cucumber purée together with double cream. □ Chill. □ Serve in bowls.

Parsnip and Rhubarb Soup

This soup made the perfect ending to a disastrous day. Disaster started in my favourite antique shop in Framlingham's Double Street when I decided to buy a slightly cracked, blue dinner service to ring the changes with my stalwart Red Aves. I misheard the price and found it was five times dearer than I thought. I was too late to visit Mr. Pinney's shop at Orford to pick up my supply of his delectable smoked cod's roe. Instead I found myself in Woodbridge in the rain. A friendly greengrocer unlocked his door to sell me the first of the season's sodden rhubarb, for a pie the next day. I also bought a couple of pounds of parsnips for soup that night. Back home my mind fused on one of my more inspirational culinary combinations: a parsnip-with-rhubarb soup. It worked.

1 large onion, sliced
3 oz unsalted butter
3 lb parsnips, peeled and sliced
2 stems young rhubarb
Brown sugar (optional)
Lemon juice (optional)
1½ pt chicken stock

Sweat onion in butter and add sliced parsnips, peeled and cored. □ Turn in the butter for 5 minutes and add rhubarb, sliced. (If your rhubarb is oversharp, add a little brown sugar; if too sweet, a little lemon juice). □ Pour in chicken stock (seasoning cubes will suffice) and simmer until tender. □ Liquidise, return to heat and season.

13

Broad Bean Soup

I have had lots of friends who are Jews, but none of them has been really Orthodox — so there has never been any problem about food. But I have a habit which can cause me trouble: I am sympathetic and like a chameleon often adopt the characteristics of the people I am talking to. Some of my best friends have taken me for Jewish — once I was even invited to write a food column for *The Jewish Chronicle*. So when Lenny sat down to supper and I placed before him my broad bean soup, it did not even occur to me that the bacon in it would be as much a mortal sin as . . . well there's really very little that would nowadays affect a Roman Catholic. The problem was that he had recently married, and Miriam, his wife, was as strict about dietary laws as a diabetic. Now she never lets him eat with me.

8 oz rindless streaky bacon
2 oz unsalted butter
4 oz sliced onion
2 lb 'podded weight' beans
2 pt chicken stock
4 slices green bacon
Butter
Garlic

Let bacon slowly sweat in a heavy pan. □ Add unsalted butter and onion and cook until translucent. □ Blanch beans, and then skin. □ Add the beans to the onion, add chicken stock and simmer until tender. □ Liquidise, reheat, check seasoning, and serve sprinkled with chopped lean, green bacon fried crisp with garlic.

Carrot and Orange Soup

It was Victor Spinetti talking on the wireless, who declared that in the country he could never buy any fresh vegetables and was glad to be once more an Underground ride away from Covent Garden. He was spouting these opinions before the pick-your-own industry boomed, but even so — for such a gregarious fellah — he must have led a peculiarly insular country life. Gladly, I have experienced the opposite. From my early days in Suffolk, and even after my own vegetable garden was carved out of solid couch grass, my doorstep would be strewn with gifts from neighbours. Last Saturday, Mr. Greenhard — who is a genius at digging out my ground elder — left a basket of perfect carrots (as well as onions, peas and shallots). I decided to make the carrots into a soup for lunch the next day. The soup had to be sophisticated in flavour. For the friend, called Blaze, who was to be the chief guest, had travelled far with a clutch of Scottish deerhounds and would not be refreshed with anything less than the unusual. It was a great success with the sophisticated and the unsophisticated.

2 lb carrots
2 oz unsalted butter
1 crushed clove garlic
Can of concentrated, frozen orange juice
1 pt chicken stock
Juice of 1 lemon
Brown sugar
Double cream

15

Scrape and roughly slice carrots.
□ Sauté gently for 5 minutes in butter with crushed garlic. □ Add contents of orange juice and chicken stock plus lemon juice. □ Simmer gently until the carrots are tender. □ Now liquidise and return to the heat. □ Check the seasoning. The soup should have a sharp taste, but add a little brown sugar if too sharp and more lemon juice if not sharp enough. □ Serve in bowls and Catherine wheel double cream over the surface. Can be served hot or chilled.

Ripe Mango Soup

The Witty American Author was to spend a short weekend at my Suffolk retreat and I sought an unusual starter for Saturday's light lunch. I found it in the pawpaw. But my ethnic hunt for the pawpaw in Caledonian Road's polyglot shops was a failure, so I bought the not-too-dissimilar mango instead. This tropical fruit varies in size and shape from something like an avocado pear to a kidney-shaped water melon. Its skin is more florid than was WC Fields', but its juicy orange flesh is delicate and fragrant. I wanted it as a first course, and had bought expensive limes to tingle-up the oversweet fruit with their freshly-squeezed juices dribbled over its cut surface. But the best laid plans . . . there were not enough halved mangoes for the number invited, so

I experimented and came up with a soup that proved to be simply delicious. Incidentally, the WAA arrived without his wit, save 'If that was a light lunch then I suppose his snack will be Moby Dick on toast.'

2 medium-sized mangoes
1 cucumber
Juice of 2 limes or lemons
1 tsp salt
10 fl oz double cream
Grated lemon peel

Scoop out the flesh from two ripe mangoes. □ Blend with unpeeled cucumber, the juice of limes, or lemons, and salt. □ Combine with whipped double cream and chill. □ Serve with lemon peel grated over the surface.

Pigeon Soup

I have succumbed completely to country ways and have gone shooting with a gun. My conversion to the mass murder of the birds of the air came when one of my gardeners, Cratfield, inherited a sum of money and left. It had been a neat arrangement: Nick took care of the lawns, Cratfield the vegetables and the hedges, and I saw to the herbaceous and tree and shrub planting. Suddenly I had to take on the care of the quarter-acre vegetable garden as well. I took a paternal pride in the peas and beans and the developing cabbage and calabrese. Then came the pigeon

17

invasion. Nothing would deter them. I took to shouting and throwing stones, but eventually I had to turn to the gun. They fell before my blasts like cardboard cutouts at a funfair. With my freezer filling with birds, I had to find new means of cooking them. Here is a special way I devised.

1 onion
1 oz unsalted butter
1 clove garlic
2 pigeons
2 pt chicken stock
Bouquet garni
½ orange
3 oz raisins
Fécule (potato flour)
Seasoning

Slice onion and cook in unsalted butter until it begins to sweat. □ Add crushed garlic and in this mixture turn pigeons, previously dredged with seasoned flour. □ Add chicken stock, bouquet garni, orange, raisins, and bring to the boil. □ Simmer for 1½ hours. □ When cool, discard skins, remove every fragment of flesh and return to the cooking liquor with all the other ingredients. □ Liquidise. □ Reheat. It should be of a fairly thick consistency. □ Test for seasoning. □ Serve with either plain live yoghurt or peach and redcurrant yoghourt trailed over the surface.

Lettuce Soup

Aunt Belinda's size belied the prettiness of her name. She was as big and fat as any old Bertha and she never stopped eating. She tried to keep her enormous appetite secret. 'No, Harold, she would say to my mother's brother (whose name anyway was Harri), 'you enjoy your steak and kidney pie. I will have just a little lettuce and Ryvita!' But we all had to subscribe to the lie that she ate hardly enough to keep a bird alive. 'A vulture?' I inquired once: and for a whole week I was given double rations of lettuce as a punishment. Even today I flush green at the thought of raw lettuce.

> 1 cucumber
> 3 oz butter
> 1 sliced onion
> 2 shredded cos/cabbage lettuces
> Handful of parsley
> 1½ pt chicken stock
> ½ pt milk
> Seasoning
> Soy sauce

Sauté a sliced, unpeeled cucumber in butter with sliced onion and add shredded cos or cabbage lettuces plus parsley. ☐ Cover with chicken stock and milk. ☐ Season and simmer for 5 minutes. ☐ Blend and serve hot, garnished with diced fried cucumber seasoned with soy sauce.

Mediterranean Fish Soup

Helen now lives partly in Switzerland and partly in America, and I miss her inordinately. This soup is one she devised.

12 oz mullet, whiting and plaice
1 large onion
6 Tbs olive oil
1 clove garlic
15-16 oz tin tomatoes
2 level Tbs tomato paste
1 heaped tsp chopped parsley
1½ pt fish stock/water
¼ pt dry white wine
1 bay leaf
Large piece of lemon peel
Slices of skinned tomatoes
Few peeled prawns

Clean, fillet and skin mullet, whiting and plaice; use the trimmings and bones as base for fish stock. □ Cut fillets diagonally into 2in pieces. □ Finely chop onion. □ Heat olive oil in a heavy-based pan and cook the onion in this until soft, but not browned. □ Crush and add garlic, fry for a minute or two before adding tomatoes in their juice, tomato paste and chopped parsley. □ Mix together and simmer slowly for 15 minutes. □ Add fish, fish stock or water, dry white wine, bay leaf and lemon peel, □ Bring back to the simmer, cover with a lid and cook slowly for 20 minutes. □ Discard bay leaf and lemon peel. □ Season and leave the soup to cool slightly. □ Remove one piece of fish for each serving and keep warm. ☐ Liquidise the rest, along with the contents of the pan, until blended to a smooth creamy consistency. ☐ Stir in cream and reheat soup without bringing it to the boil ☐ Place one piece of fish in each individual bowl and pour over the soup. ☐ Float slices of skinned tomatoes, garnished with peeled prawns, on top of each bowl.

Turnip and Watercress Soup

A year last Christmas I was having lunch with an editor who proudly presented, as a first course, turnip soup. It was nondescript and faintly unpleasant. Luckily, I knew her well enough to discuss the reason for its failure. The recipe she had used I knew well and it is good: but it relied on the delicate spring turnips that appear in May. For her, I have devised a soup made from the coarser winter vegetable that could be served on even the grandest occasion.

4 oz unsalted butter
9 chopped-up large turnips
1 sliced onion
2 crushed cloves garlic
2 pt chicken stock
1 bay leaf
Sea salt
Freshly ground black pepper
3 bunches of watercress
Crumbled Stilton cheese

In butter cook slowly for 15 minutes, without browning, turnips together with onion and garlic. ☐ Add chicken stock, bay leaf, sea salt and freshly ground black pepper. ☐ Simmer for 15 minutes. ☐ Now add large bunches of watercress and simmer for a further 7½ minutes. ☐ Purée in the blender, and thin with more stock, if necessary. ☐ Serve in soup plates on which you have first spread a layer of crumbled Stilton cheese. ☐ Alternatively, blend the cheese with a little cream and stuff this mixture into choux balls and serve them piled on a plate for guests to help themselves.

Melon Soup

I have never considered melon good enough for a first course at dinner, whether it be Ogen or Charentais. And I have never been able to decide whether Charentais or Ogen has the better flavour — although a week in Israel, where growing the Ogen is akin to a religion, tipped my balance in favour of the Charentais. 'In 1947', said our guide, 'Israel was created' . . . as though the land was a postscript that an absent-minded God added on a belated eighth day. 'Then we irrigated and grew lemons and oranges and Ogen melons and more Ogen melons and more Ogen melons . . .' Now, I do like a little melon for breakfast and this is how my melon soup happened. My assistant, Paul, was to come to dinner and he is besotted with melons. So I experimented with a soup made with the half Ogen left over from breakfast time. It is absolutely the best cold soup I have served.

1 melon
Grated peel and juice of 2 oranges
Grated peel and juice of 1 lemon
1 Tbs brown sugar
Ground ginger

De-seed and peel melon. ☐ Blend flesh with grated peel, orange and lemon juice and brown sugar. ☐ Stir in ground ginger to taste ☐ Serves four.

Cream of Artichoke Soup

The lady-of-the-manor who sold me my home in Suffolk taught me a lot about country ways, including an appreciation of that odd-looking root, the Jerusalem artichoke. She had me to lunch and in response to my expressed delight at its flavour she uttered, 'They are topinambours, my dear. I learned about them in Paris. The English serve them badly overboiled and in a flour-paste of a white sauce. You should parboil them for five minutes, roll in seasoned flour, toss over heat in melted butter and bake with more butter and perhaps a squeeze of lemon juice'.

1½ lb Jerusalem artichokes
3 oz butter
1 large sliced onion
¼ cucumber, sliced
3 pt chicken stock
Bunch of parsley
Seasoning
10 fl oz double cream
Yoghourt/crumbled Stilton cheese

Peel artichokes and place in large pan with melted butter. ☐ Add onion and cucumber, and turn in butter over a low heat for 5 minutes. ☐ Add chicken stock (if using stock cubes, make them at three-quarters strength) and bring to the simmer. ☐ Add parsley.
☐ Simmer for about 20 minutes until vegetables are tender. ☐ Remove parsley and liquidise. ☐ Check for seasoning and chill. ☐ Just before serving, stir in double cream and trail a little yoghourt over surface of each bowl or some crumbled Stilton cheese. ☐ Serves 8.

FIRST COURSES

Brundish Onion Tart

Brigitte Serre, the wife of a French colleague, served me her onion tart as the first course at a dinner in their flat in the rather smart Passy area of Paris. She is charming and blonde, with three flaxen-haired children. After dinner, while we settled down to a cognac, Brigitte went off to a parent/teachers' association meeting. The tart was the thing which impressed me most. Until then I had considered my own version of this ubiquitous dish *très schön*, but hers was the better. Lighter, with crisper pastry. She prebaked the case and poured in the filling — which was perhaps too runny. Since then I have experimented and I have now come up with an onion tart that satisfies me.

1 lb onions
2 oz butter
1 dsp soft brown sugar
Juice of 1 lemon
Shortcrust pastry
8 fl oz double cream
2 eggs
Seasoning

Peel and very finely slice onions. □ Sweat in butter with soft brown sugar and lemon juice. □ Meanwhile, line an 8in flan ring with rich shortcrust pastry rolled out very thinly. □ Drain the onions and combine with double cream beaten well with eggs and seasoned. □ Pour into flan case, dot with butter, and bake at 425 deg.F. (Gas Mark 7) for 5 minutes then at 375 deg.F. (Gas Mark 5) for 25 minutes.

Salmon and Avocado Terrine

The Miller Howe at Bowness on Windermere is on everybody's gourmet map as an essential part of a Lakeland visit. I first went there years back so that I could write about it in my restaurant column. Then the dining room was the front parlour. It is glamorously tiered now and drops to a wall of sheer glass looking out over the lake. At 8.30 precisely the lights dim dramatically and the show is on. The maestro and head-cook-and-bottle-washer is John Tovey (the pair of peacocks which once strutted the terrace have folded up their tails, their splendour dimmed by John's culinary displays, and disappeared). John is a great food enthusiast and his meals, which were exciting when I first visited his hotel, have done nothing but improve since. Recently, after everybody had gone to bed, I sat in a high-backed chair in the conservatory, lit only by a 'safety' blue lamp and sipped brandy, quietly toasting John and his success.

8 eggs
2 Tbs onion salt
1 Tbs caster sugar
1 lb smoked salmon
1 tin clams
2 level Tbs gelatine
½ pt white wine
6 avocado pears
2 tsp salt
2 tsp onion juice
4 tsp Worcester sauce
½ pt home-made mayonnaise
½ pt double cream

27

Beat egg yolks to a 'ribbon' in your mixer with onion salt and caster sugar. □ Liquidise smoked salmon with clams and pass through a sieve. □ Fold into the yolk mixture, and then fold into 8 stiffly beaten egg whites. □ Spoon into prepared Swiss-roll tin and bake for 15 minutes at 360 deg.F. (Gas Mark 4). □ Meanwhile, dissolve gelatine in white wine. □ Scoop out the flesh of avocado pears, and break up with a 'K' beater, then whisk with the wine, salt, onion juice, Worcester sauce, mayonnaise and double cream until comparatively smooth. □ When the salmon is cool, invert from the tin and spread over it the avocado mixture, rolling as you would a Swiss-roll. □ Chill. □ Serves 8.

Larry Grayson's Smoked Haddock

I had been asked to interview Larry Grayson, the host of television's 'The Generation Game' but before doing that I thought I had better watch the programme. Halfway through, I flagged. I thought I would simply poach an egg, but then my indomitable spirit rose and I produced a new dish in a flash. It serves as a good starter for six or as a main course for four.

1 whole Finnan Haddock
1 small onion
1½ oz unsalted butter
1 apple
1 clove garlic
2 tsp double cream
8 oz tin Italian peeled tomatoes
Juice of 1 lemon
Pepper
Spinach, green salad
Bread
Lemon

Place haddock skin side up beneath a hot grill; the skin can then be removed easily. □ Cut across into pieces. □ Sauté finely sliced onion in unsalted butter with a peeled, cored and finely chopped apple and a crushed clove of garlic. □ Now turn the haddock in this mixture for a few minutes, add double cream, tomatoes, lemon juice and a generous amount of freshly milled pepper. □ Cook gently for 10 minutes. □ Serve as main course with spinach and a green salad. □ As a starter, pick out the bones and pour the flesh and sauce on six rounds of crustless bread sliced ½in thick which have been soaked in butter and allowed to crisp in the oven. A wedge of lemon should accompany each serving.

Tomato Cream

I am often asked by friends for a recipe to make and serve at their next dinner party. Usually they funk the effort and fall back on their well tried — *petits pôts de chocolat*. Or they can be like my friend Betty, who was delighted at my suggestion of turning her braising steak into an approximation of a carbonnade by layering it with onions and casseroling it in the essential brown ale. She rang me next day to tell me how successful the meal had been. 'The beef was simply delicious' she gushed 'and I did exactly as you said, except I didn't bother to add the beer, darling!' However, she is a very old and dear friend so when her ambition was to serve a meal using only my recipes, I protected both our reputations by cooking the food myself.

24 oz canned tomatoes
2 tsp brown sugar
Salt
Pepper
4 cloves
2 bay leaves
Juice of 1 lemon
5 fl oz vodka
10 fl oz double cream
Tomato, lemon slices

Simmer together for 10 minutes canned tomatoes with brown sugar, pepper, salt, cloves, bay leaves, lemon juice and vodka. ☐ Sieve, then freeze until mushy. ☐ Fold in stiffly beaten double cream. ☐ Freeze overnight. ☐ Serve in tall glasses with tomato and lemon slices.

Pheasant Terrine

I have given the Christmas cake an extra spiking of cognac and looked over the puddings to make sure there is no mould. I have admired my shelves of peaches and cherries in brandy, the pears in kirsch and the humbler (but still delicious) spiced prunes and spiced crab apples. The goose is in the freezer, the Bradenham ham on order at Harrods. Crackers from Fortnums, Carlsbad plums and crystallised fruits from Framlingham's Carley & Webb. I have earmarked in the hedges the best rose branches with the brightest hips; pulled the tallest bullrushes and sprayed them with lacquer and chosen the varieties of ivy and holly which will soon bedeck the house. For this is to be a joyous Christmas and with that feeling of anticipation I shall now make a pheasant terrine, to be frozen until Christmas is here (leave the making for a fortnight and it will keep without freezing providing you run a good ½in of lard over the top, wrap up in foil and store in the refrigerator).

8 bay leaves
8 juniper berries
1 level tsp salt
6 peppercorns
½ wine-glass brandy
Brace of pheasants
1 lb veal
1 lb belly pork
¾ lb streaky bacon
1 tsp basil, thyme, marjoram
Salt, pepper

In a large bowl, mix together 4 bay leaves, crushed juniper berries, salt, peppercorns and brandy. □ Cut the meat in thin slices from pheasants and leave for 8-10 hours in the marinade. □ Turn several times. □ Mince veal with the cleaned liver, heart and kidneys from the pheasants. □ Mince belly pork. □ Line a 2pt terrine with rindless streaky bacon slices. □ Strain the marinade from the pheasant. □ Lay half the minced pork on the bacon, followed by a layer of veal. □ Sprinkle each layer with mixed basil, thyme, marjoram, salt and pepper. □ Lay the pheasant meat over the veal, pour the strained marinade over and top with the other half of the pork. □ Cover the top with more streaky bacon and bay leaves, and protect the terrine with buttered greaseproof paper before putting on the lid. □ Place in a bain marie and set in a preheated oven at 375 deg.F. (Gas Mark 5) for 1½ hours or until the juices run clear yellow. □ About 15 minutes before cooking is completed, remove the lid and greaseproof paper to allow the top of the terrine to brown. □ Cool for 30 minutes. □ Cover the terrine with clean greaseproof paper and weight down with a 2 lb weight set on a board.

Cauliflower Timbale

I was not allowed to be choosy. 'It is only the working class who indulge themselves that way,' quoth Mother, 'and you can always recognise them because they never like mushrooms, offal or coffee.' This edict nearly ricocheted when, by this standard, I wrongly classified one of Lord Astor's grandsons — but since he was flattered by the mistake, all proved to be well. But she (my mother) did have a fad: she declared that cauliflower was only palatable if eaten raw. Independently, I had always agreed with her until I discovered the delight of eating the boiled florets served as a timbale.

6 oz rich shortcrust pastry
1 cauliflower
8 fl oz cream
2 eggs
3 oz Gruyère
Salt
Pepper
Scrape of nutmeg
Butter

Line an 8in flan ring with shortcrust pastry and in it arrange the blanched florets from a large cauliflower. □ Beat together cream, eggs, 2 ounces finely grated Gruyère, salt, pepper and nutmeg. □ Pour over the cauliflower. □ Dot with butter and further ounce of Gruyère. □ Place in oven at 425 deg. F. (Gas Mark 7); after 10 minutes reduce to 350 deg.F. (Gas Mark 4) for a further 20 minutes.

33

Snails en Croûte

It takes 200 snails to equal the protein value of a pound of rare Scotch beef, but at the prices restaurants are charging there is no danger that our taste for this delicacy will destroy the species. Snails are not a French prerogative; English country folk have often cooked and eaten them, picking them out of their shells like winkles. The common garden snail is a land gasteropod of the genus *Helix*, of which there are more than 112 species — making it the second largest group in the animal kingdom. The garden snail, *Helix aspersa*, is not so highly regarded as *Helix pomatia*, the Roman snail, a meatier morsel more often sold in restaurants, and both are dwarfed by the giant African snail, *Achatina*, which can be 8in long. You can actually catch and eat your local snails. But I buy a tin which holds 24 to 26 snails and serves six.

24-26 tinned snails
Puff pastry
Dry white wine
½ onion
3 cloves garlic
1 Tbs brandy
Seasoning
3 oz butter
1 oz double cream
Egg glaze
Horseradish sauce

Make puff pastry from 8 oz each of flour and butter (ready-made puff pastry will suffice). □ Cook the snails in the liquor in which they are canned or, preferably, drain the liquor and cook in dry white wine. □ Add to the cooking liquor the sliced onion, 1 crushed clove of garlic, brandy and seasoning. □ Cook for half an hour and set aside to cool. □ Crush 2 cloves of garlic into butter, combine with double cream and chill well. □ Roll out the pastry very thinly and cut into 12 rounds with a 3in cutter shape. □ Brush six of the rounds with egg white and place 4 snails and one-sixth of the butter mixture on each round. □ Wet the edges of all the pastry circles, place the remaining rounds of pastry on top of the bases and press well together to seal. □ Place on a greased baking tray and decorate the top of each pastry case with shapes cut from the rolled out surplus pastry. □ Swill the baking tray with cold water, brush the pastry with an egg glaze and place in an oven preheated to 500 deg.F. (Gas Mark 9). Lower immediately to 400 deg.F. (Gas Mark 6) and cook for 20 to 25 minutes, until well-risen and golden. □ Serve each with a tablespoon of horseradish sauce.

Insalata

The occasion was when I went on tour with Mother and she was due to appear at La Scala. I awoke on the day of the performance to find our bags packed and Mother flurrying me to the airport. In answer to my querulous 'Why are we leaving?' she said, 'The city is full of cakes and very bad for a pubescent boy.' The papers next morning told me she had quarrelled with the musical director and had walked out on her contract. (Later Grandmama told me the real truth, which was that she was in bad voice and that the Musetta to her Mimi was an emerging star in superb voice and *that* Mother could never tolerate.) We stopped over in Rome and took lunch. To begin with she called for leeks: 'Nero ate them daily, for his voice.' But she had to be content with asparagus: 'They were Augustus Caesar's favourite.' I ordered *Insalata de Funghi*, which with adaptations I have often used since as a starter, as a salad or as a main course at luncheon.

8 oz mushrooms
Olive oil
Juice of 1 lemon
2 cloves garlic
6 shakes Tabasco
1 tsp caster sugar
1 tsp salt
1 tsp black pepper
5 oz shrimps
¼ pt double cream
Chopped parsley

Finely slice mushrooms into a serving dish, saturate with olive oil and stir in the lemon juice, crushed cloves, Tabasco, caster sugar, salt and black pepper. ☐ Chill for 1 hour. ☐ Now stir in shrimps and double cream and sprinkle copiously with finely chopped parsley. ☐ For a vegetable course leave out the shrimps and add black olives. As a main course add flaked crab or lobster.

Mousse Paulas

The holder of the title International Chef of the Year in 1979 (there were entrants from everywhere, including Japan and Malta) was Paul Brady of the Royal County Hotel, Durham (the hostelry with the balcony from which Sir Harold Wilson used to wave to the assembled miners at their annual gala). Paul Brady is an exceptional *chef-de-cuisine*. He provides a master plan of 21 main-course variations of fish, meat and chicken dishes for his brigade of chefs so that no guest staying for a few weeks need have any dish duplicated. I have eaten my way through every variation and I have not found a failure. For you I have chosen a starter, *Mousse Paulas* (named after his daughter) from the meal which won him his title.

1 bunch of watercress
Bicarbonate of soda
4 large globe artichoke hearts
4 fl oz mayonnaise
4 fl oz double cream
8 oz smoked salmon
3 dsp powdered gelatine
Lemon juice
Oatcakes

Blanch watercress in boiling water, with a little bicarbonate of soda to keep it green. ☐ Refresh and dry and give it a twirl through a blender. ☐ Simmer artichoke hearts in salted water (with a little lemon juice added), then purée and beat into half the mayonnaise and whipped double cream. ☐ Combine with the watercress mixture. ☐ Now purée smoked salmon and then beat into the remaining whipped cream and mayonnaise. ☐ On to the surface of a saucerful of hot water, sprinkle powdered gelatine between the two mixtures, mixing it in thoroughly. ☐ Check seasoning. ☐ Divide the mixtures between four oiled 3in soufflé moulds, putting in the artichoke mixture first and allowing it to chill for 30 minutes before adding the salmon mixture. ☐ Leave overnight. ☐ Turn out and decorate tops with miniscule diamonds of razor-thin truffles or smoked salmon. ☐ Serve with 1in wide hot oatcakes.

MAIN COURSES

Leveret in a Pot

There is a richness to jugged hare that even the best brought-up people might find off-putting — especially if they learn that an essential ingredient is the last-minute incorporation of the hare's blood. Pity, though, the grown-up who finds himself deprived because of an underdeveloped taste in food. This recipe came into being because of such an acquaintance who 'hated hare'. She had never tasted it, and was not told what the casserole held until after a second helping. It is one of the most refreshing meat dishes I have made, and can be served quite safely to even a die-hard hater of hare, jugged.

1 leveret
2 onions
Oil
Butter
Seasoned flour
½ pt white wine
½ pt fresh orange juice
Seasoning cube
1 bay leaf
5 Tbs raspberry jam
Juice of 2 lemons
1 lb baby carrots
6 oz whole mushrooms
Rice
Sweetcorn from 3 cobs
Black pepper

Joint the leveret, coat with seasoned flour and brown in 2 tablespoons of oil and butter. □ Sweat onions in the same fat until translucent. □ Pour over equal quantities of hot white wine and fresh orange juice to cover. □ Add seasoning cube, bay leaf, raspberry jam (sieved) and the lemon juice. □ Bring to the simmer and cook in the oven at 350 deg.F. (Gas Mark 3) for 1½ hours. □ Add baby carrots and mushrooms and cook for 30 minutes longer until all is tender. □ Serve with rice which has first been boiled for 11 minutes and then drained and finished in butter, with sweetcorn taken from the blanched cobs. □ Just before serving grind a generous amount of black pepper over the rice.

Suffolk Stew

'I am 70 tomorrow,' said my jobbing gardener 'and my mother be turned 90.' Uninterrupted by my muttered 'Gracious,' he went on, 'My father died when he was 96. A marvellous man. He only did "taking" work — that is piece-work — and when he "flashed" a field he used to have a bill-hook in each hand. Twelve children he brought up on a pound a week. Stone-ground bread and cheese kept us going in the fields all day. But on Saturday we always had stew. I'll get the way she made it from my mother.' And he did, and very good it is too on a cold February day.

41

2 oz lentils
1 oz haricot beans
1 oz pearl barley
2 large potatoes
1 large turnip
4 carrots
4 onions
Best end of neck of lamb
2 bay leaves
Salt
Pepper
Handful of parsley/mixed herbs
3 pt water

Soak lentils, haricot beans and pearl barley in cold water overnight. □ Peel and roughly chop potatoes, turnip, carrots, onions and deposit in a large saucepan. □ Trim excess fat from the best end of neck of lamb and cut into chops. □ Add to the vegetables, with bay leaves, salt, pepper and a handful of parsley (or mixed herbs). □ Drain the lentils etc. and add. □ Top with the water. □ Simmer for 3 hours.

Summer Terrine

Because I loved Antibes I wished that I had scurried through France with the reputed fervour of the American package tourist. 'We are now bypassing Chartres, folks. And you can tell your grandchildren that, had we stopped, you would have seen some of the finest stained glass in the world.' But on my dash South I had lingered here and there, entranced with every blue and red plaque that spelled *Les Routiers*. But there I was on the last of my five days in Antibes and committed to visiting a couple of English exiles. It took me two hours to find their villa, and I was bad tempered. But my temper dissipated immediately I saw the staunch cricket-playing Roland immersed in a game of *boules* with the villagers. On the terrace, overlooking a distant Nice, Patricia served me chilled Chambéry. We ate in a vine-clad arbour a terrine adapted from a recipe of my mother's.

1 lb chicken
1 lb veal
1 lb lean pork
½ pt dry white wine
1 clove garlic
½ onion, sliced
1 bay leaf
2 Tbs olive oil
Black pepper , sea salt
$\frac{3}{4}$ lb thinly sliced
¾ lb rindless streaky, bacon
2 Tbs chopped parsley
5 fl oz sweet sherry
Finely sliced red peppers
4 oz flaked almonds

43

Slice finely chicken, veal and lean pork into a marinade of dry white wine, garlic, onion, bay leaf, olive oil, black pepper and sea salt. □ Leave for 8 hours, turning from time to time. □ Line a terrine with rindless streaky bacon. □ Remove the meat from the marinade, mince a quarter finely and stir into this mince chopped parsley and sweet sherry. □ Spread half of this mince on the base of the terrine and cover with a layer of finely sliced red peppers and flaked almonds. □ On this arrange half of the sliced meat, sprinkle with salt and pepper and then spread over the rest of the minced meat. □ Now repeat the almond and red pepper layer and then the balance of the sliced meat. □ Season. □ Cover with kitchen foil and bake in a bain-marie at 335 deg.F. (Gas Mark 3) for 2½ hours. □ Cool. □ Weight overnight and serve with a salad of apples and lettuce leaves.

Lamb Chops Adrian

I am not very good to unexpected guests. A few years back I was quite ruthless: particularly with a couple who appeared while I was pottering in the garden. I escorted them around the beds until I manoeuvred them to the gate, where I wished them a happy return journey. Somewhat taken aback, they blurted out: 'Well, at least we thought you'd offer us a drink.' I was in and out of the house in a trice and offered them a glass of water. Nowadays I have mellowed a little and secretly enjoy the challenge of turning out a full-blown meal with no notice. But in my not-so-well-stocked London flat, this can be difficult: the other day a friend really in need turned up unexpectedly, and I felt a couple of grilled lamb chops would be inadequate solace. So I concocted a dish which sent him off replete, if not happy. The easy recipe can now provide the basis for many an inexpert cook's dinner party.

8 lamb chops
2 Tbs olive oil
1 chopped onion
4 oz tin of button mushrooms
8 oz tin Italian tomatoes
1 Tbs dark chunky marmalade

Sauté the lamb chops in olive oil with finely chopped onion, add button mushrooms (drained), tin of peeled tomatoes, and (its secret) dark chunky marmalade. ☐ Season and simmer for 15 minutes.

Steaks

Steaks really are not my forte and I found it disconcerting when Aunt Blodwen's voice emerged from the past on the telephone. 'Your Uncle Edwin and I are coming to London and would like to see you after this very long time.' Ever polite, and ignoring the fact they were not really relations at all (the

Welsh have a curious habit of making any older acquaintance an Auntie — especially if female), I invited them to dinner. 'That's lovely of you' gushed 'Aunt' Blodwen. 'And since you're now such a fine cook would you give us steak? That would be a great treat.' I seemed doomed to serve my anathema — grilled steaks. My butcher had no fillet, but had rump ('It is beautifully hung, Friesian, with flavour and tenderness.') At the very last moment I rebelled, but I was delighted to hear 'Aunt' Blodwen say, 'There's a lovely way to cook steak. Is it difficult to do?'

1 lb rump steak
1 small onion
2 oz butter
2 fl oz olive oil
2 Tbs warm brandy
5 fl oz double cream
1 level dsp tomato paste
1 level dsp brown sugar
Wine vinegar
Lea & Perrins
Seasoning
Cabbage
Soy sauce

Cut rump or fillet steak into approximately 3in by ⅛in slices.
☐ Melt butter and add olive oil, and in it sweat the finely chopped onion.
☐ Throw in steak and turn until coloured. ☐ Flambé with warm brandy. ☐ Pour in double cream, season and then add tomato paste, brown sugar and wine vinegar, and add Lea & Perrins to taste. ☐ Cook for 1 minute. ☐ Serve with cabbage, quickly boiled, drained and turned in cream with dashes of soy sauce.

Skate with Green Pepper Sauce

I can number on one hand those of my friends who take to skate. It can even appear on a menu as *Raie au beurre noir* and others still shy from it as instinctively as they would from a disturbed adder. Yet it is such a delicious fish. I have pondered on its bad points: its extreme ugliness and the fact that its skin is so horny that fishermen wear protective gloves and use pincers to tear away the outer covering to reveal the delicate, edible wings. So I have come up with a solution which has converted three out of five who previously hated skate.

Skate
1 dsp unsalted butter
1 dsp aromatic green peppers
3 oz double cream
Juice of ½ lemon
1 dsp brown sugar
Green salad

Melt unsalted butter over a low heat and into this crush aromatic green peppers from the tin. ☐ Add double cream, lemon juice and brown sugar. ☐ Cook for 5 minutes and force through a fine sieve. ☐ Return to the heat, add a little salt and a little more cream or crushed peppers (in which case you must sieve again) according to your taste. ☐ Pour a little over each wing of cooked skate which is cooked in 5 minutes in water coming to a simmer. ☐ Serve with a green salad sweetly dressed.

Saxon Pudding

Our Calvinistic, puritanical and just darned awkward Scottish housekeeper, Aggie, found solace with a minister in an obscure part of Western Argyllshire. She is still viciously alive and is likely to descend on me with the venom of a Walt Disney Witch if I tell of her exact whereabouts. Among other things, the minister taught her to appreciate game — of the furred and feathered kind. Grouse was the bird she served when the house offered its best; but once when I had taken ill and had stayed over for a week or two, she served me Saxon Pudding — an unusual combination of steak and partridge cooked in a basin within a suet crust.

Partridge
Seasoned flour
¼ lb rump steak
2 oz mushrooms
Parsley
Pinch of dried mixed herbs
5 fl oz burgundy
Chicken stock
Pastry

Joint a partridge and roll in seasoned flour with rump steak. ☐ Cut in 1in cubes and place in the basin along with coarsely chopped mushrooms and finely chopped parsley and mixed herbs. ☐ Pour over burgundy and top up with chicken stock. ☐ Cover with a pastry lid and buttered greaseproof paper, and then tie around a cloth. ☐ Place in a pan of boiling water and steam for 3 hours.

Baked Beans

I dislike the mealy, sweet taste of tinned baked beans as much as I like its origins. The baked bean was a rib-sticking part of our 17th century diet, which emigrated to America with the Puritans. The dish was their godsend, its long cooking enabling them to put it in the oven on a Saturday night and serve it piping hot on workless Sunday: their version became known as Boston Baked Beans. My way is a cross between the English and the American version with a touch of the French cassoulet thrown in — they are similar peasant dishes with the bean as a prime ingredient.

16 oz haricot beans
1 Tbs soft brown sugar
1 Tbs treacle
Heart of celery
1 level dsp English mustard
Black pepper
1½ lb piece of salt belly pork

Soak the haricot beans for 12 hours, place them in a marmite or deep casserole with brown sugar, treacle, cut-up leafy heart of celery, English mustard, lots of black pepper and, on top, piece of salt belly pork.
☐ Cover with water and bake overnight in an oven set at 280 deg.F. (Gas Mark 1). ☐ Next morning, check liquid and continue at same temperature till lunchtime, taking off the lid to brown the pork for the last hour. ☐ I serve the pork and beans for a meal and then freeze the rest in individual portions.

Partridge in Chocolate Sauce

When prairie methods of growing crops gained ground, the creation of vast hedgeless fields ploughed right up to the drainage ditches practically meant the near extinction of the partridge. This game bird feeds on the ripening corn and the young need the space on the fringes of the fields to dry off after our usual summer-long showers, otherwise they become chilled and die. The farmers are now allowing a smidgin more space and cover for the game bird, and the partridge is making a comeback.

4 partridges
1 oz unsalted butter
1 Tbs oil
Seasoning
12 gob-stopper sized onions
4 fl oz sherry
1 oz chocolate Menier
2 fl oz double cream

Brown the partridges in unsalted butter and oil in an ovenproof dish. □ Season and roast at 450 deg.F. (Gas Mark 7), covered for 25 minutes. □ Half way through cooking, glaze onions in butter and add to dish. □ Remove partridges and deglaze the pan with sherry and allow to cook until liquid thickens slightly, then stir in finely grated chocolate Menier and double cream. □ Serve on ½in rounds of bread, soaked in melted butter and crisped in the oven. Surround by the onions and coat with sauce.

Perfect Fish and Chips

My favourite story is of a girlfriend who wanted to serve a dinner to impress me. In desperation on the morning of the feast she rang and asked me how to cook the hunk of venison she had carted back from Scotland. I asked how long it had been hung. 'Hung?' she retorted, 'It was shot! And I've kept it fresh in the refrigerator ever since.' For dinner I taught her how to make perfect fish and chips.

Old potatoes
4 pt cold water
1 dsp rock salt
4 oz flour
Pinch of salt
1 Tbs olive oil
5 fl oz cold water
1 egg-white
8 oz portions cod

Peel old potatoes thinly, cut into cylinders and then into sticks, ¼in wide, 2½in long. ☐ Soak in 4 pints cold water with rock salt for 45 minutes. ☐ Make batter with flour, salt, oil, cold water (just when using incorporate stiffly beaten egg white). ☐ Heat a deep chip pan one-third full of oil to 340 deg. F., add thoroughly dried chips, and cook for 4½ minutes. ☐ Drain. ☐ Dip portions of cod through batter and slip into oil at 385 deg.F. ☐ Cook for 3 minutes, switch off heat and in a further 4 minutes fish will be cooked. ☐ Reheat oil to 396 deg.F., add chips and cook for 1 minute. ☐ Drain.

Pâté de Canard en Croûte

It is not the horses I object to at point-to-points, but the people: the females who straddle the backs of stationwagons dispensing warm gin and congealed chicken and limp lettuce leaves while their spouses stand by effetely, gazing into the distance. How civilised it would be, on a brisk March day, for someone to warm my belly — as well as the cockles of my heart — with a hot turnip soup, poured steamingly from a Thermos flask; then to let me wolf through a *pâté de canard en croûte*, helped down by a Taittinger Brut, and then contentedly pig myself on peaches in brandy. The cheeses refused, I should be ready to accept a generous Delamain. After all one needs sustenance to endure these so Very Physical Sports.

Boned young duck
1 tsp mixed salt, pepper, powdered mace
4 fl oz brandy
4 fl oz sherry
1 lb minced belly pork
1 lb minced veal
1 Tbs onion
1 clove garlic
2 tsp mixed salt, pepper, thyme
2 eggs
4 oz butter
1¼ lb shortcrust pastry

Lay duck on the table, skin side down, rather like a sheepskin rug. ☐ Chop the duck's liver and place evenly over the duck with mixed salt, pepper and powdered mace. ☐ Sprinkle over brandy and sherry. ☐ Mix belly pork, veal and grated onion and add crushed garlic clove, mixed salt, pepper and powdered thyme. ☐ Mix in beaten eggs. ☐ Roll the stuffing to the shape of the bird and place it on the duck. ☐ Bring the skin up and around, restoring the duck shape. Sew the edges together with a trussing needle using fine string. ☐ Melt butter in a heavy frying pan and brown the duck on all sides. ☐ Cool. ☐ Roll out shortcrust pastry to a thick circle and put the duck on its back in the centre; bring up the pastry, wetting the edges and patting firmly into shape. ☐ Glaze and decorate. ☐ Cut a small steam hole and bake in the middle of the preheated oven at 350 deg.F. (Gas Mark 4) for 2½ hours. Once it is golden protect with several thicknesses of greaseproof. ☐ Leave till the following day and serve with Cumberland sauce.

Venison Hot Pot

Regular readers will remember Aggie, our archetypal dour Scottish housekeeper, now returned to our fold, having divorced her Calvinistic

minister. For a long time, she regarded
game as a sin of the flesh, along with
playing cards, chocolates, roses, punting
and hunting. She caught me smoking at
the tender age of 14 and told me in
doomladen tones that this was a mortal sin,
adding that if Gaed intended me tae smoke
he would have put a wee 'lum' in my head.
However, recently she has learned a great
deal about game and one of her
now-favourite dishes is Venison Hot Pot. I
enjoy it and even mop up the gravy with a
bit of bread. The buck is best for eating but
is out of season (except for freezer owners)
between June and September. The doe is
quite satisfactory for this dish and is in
season from September until year's end.
The best, of course, is the Scottish red
deer, followed by the fallow and roe (from
the New Forest and elsewhere). The
choice cuts for roasting are haunch, loin,
saddle and the leg. The forequarters make
a good pie or casserole and the flank and
breast are perfect for pâtés. But the cheap
scrag end of neck and the best end are
excellent for our hot pot.

4 oz belly pork
2 bay leaves
1½ lb scrag/shoulder/
best end of venison
2 onions
2 carrots
2 turnips
4 chopped celery sticks
Celery heart
2 Tbs seasoned flour
1½ pt beef stock
Faggot of thyme and parsley
Pinch of powdered mace
3 Tbs wine vinegar

Finely dice belly pork and fry in a pan until nicely browned. □ Drain and put into the bottom of a casserole with bay leaves. □ Cut scrag, shoulder or best end of venison into 1in cubes, toss in seasoned flour and fry in the fat remaining from the pork for 8 minutes, adding a little lard if necessary.
□ Drain and put with the pork in the casserole. □ Now add to the casserole chopped onions, peeled and chopped carrots, peeled and chopped turnips, chopped sticks and heart of celery.
□ Stir any of the remaining seasoned flour into the fat in the pan to make a brown roux and now add very slowly beef stock (or tinned consommé).
□ Bring to the boil, stirring well, and simmer until it thickens. □ Pour this over the meat in the casserole and add a faggot of thyme and parsley (or a bouquet garni), powdered mace and wine vinegar (no salt — there should be sufficient in the beef stock).
□ Cover and cook in an oven heated to 325 deg.F. (Gas Mark 3) for 2½ hours or until the meat is tender.
□ After you have adjusted the seasoning, serve with green beans of any kind or leeks with rice.

Chicken Christian

It was the second anniversary of Paul's working with me as an assistant and I sought to invent a dish to mark the occasion. Smoked salmon is his delight, and on late mornings his perfect breakfast is to have it combined with scrambled eggs — especially, as so often happens, when it is accompanied by a glass or two of champagne. Something 'different' with smoked salmon seemed unlikely. Then Paul requested *Chicken Kiev* for the celebratory menu. Now this dish can be rather dull unless spiked — quite improperly — with garlic: in any case it is relegated now to the 'Scampi and Chips' class. But *Kiev* formed the basis for *Chicken Christian,* so called because Christian is Paul's given name (never used normally, for in my kitchen there can be nothing that even hints of mutiny). And the success of the dish was certain when, with the first mouthful (chicken combined with smoked salmon and oozing prawn butter) all the guests reacted by flinging their eyes to the heavens in imitation of the Bisto kids.

1 chicken
1½ oz butter
3 oz prawns
4 slices of smoked salmon
Flour
1 egg
Breadcrumbs

Remove the skinned breasts from chicken cleanly (and include the wing, which is discarded). ☐ Place between waxed paper and flatten. ☐ Pound butter with prawns, add seasoning and shape into four sticks before freezing. ☐ Cut each breast into two. ☐ Place on the breast a slice of smoked salmon and in the middle of the salmon a stick of prawn butter. Form the chicken around the butter as though it were a lollipop — a short length of the wing bone can act as a 'stick' for one. Tie top and bottom with cotton until you can master the art of so fragmenting the edges of the flattened chicken that they stay stuck together. ☐ Dip the chicken in flour, then beaten egg and then breadcrumbs. ☐ Chill for 1 hour, or freeze for 15 minutes. ☐ Repeat the process. ☐ After chilling for 1 hour, deep fry at 350 deg.F. (Gas Mark 4) for 4 minutes. ☐ Then remove the source of heat and let the 'Christians' cook in oil for a further 5 minutes.

Pheasant in Raisin Sauce

Even my butcher will under-hang pheasants. But he has also provided me with two perfect birds (hung for a full fortnight in cool weather); and until you have tasted a well-hung pheasant, then pheasant you have not tasted. Grouse,

teal, partridge — magnificent in themselves —
fade in comparison. It is like love; you
know when it happens. It certainly is not an
over-gamey quality, which can be quite
off-putting. Last season I found a pheasant
on my doorstep which I thought a kindly
neighbour had left for me. I asked the
local layer-out-of-the-dead and
pheasant-plucker to dress the bird. She
returned it dressed, saying 'Right odd
tastes you do have'. Too late I realised that
bird must have been long dead and
dragged to my doorstep by one of those
mysterious night predators who pull my
pelargoniums out of their tubs. But an
under-hung pheasant tastes as dull as
chicken crossed with a guinea fowl, and it
is served invariably with a bread sauce —
which is like seeing a double bill of The
Sound of Music and Love Story. Serve
your run-of-the-mill pheasant this way.

Brace of pheasants
4 oz stoned raisins
10 fl oz dry white wine
Peel of 1 orange
Peel of 1 lemon
Black pepper
1 level Tbs sea salt
2 onions
4 oz unsalted butter

Sauce
Chicken stock
1 bouquet garni
1 onion
Parsley
1 carrot
1 lemon
Worcester sauce
5 fl oz double cream

Steep stoned raisins overnight in dry white wine, along with the pithless peel of the orange and lemon.
☐ Grind into the vents of a brace of pheasants a generous amount of black pepper and sea salt. ☐ Push into each vent a whole onion and 2 ounces of unsalted butter. ☐ Roast breast-side down at 400 deg.F. (Gas Mark 6) for 15 minutes, and breast-side up for 10 minutes more, basting all the while. Electric stove users will need to use foil and stock, water or wine for the initial cooking. ☐ Carve up the pheasants, discard the skin, and wrap in foil.

For the sauce, crush the pheasant carcase and place in a saucepan.
☐ Cover with chicken stock plus a bouquet garni, sliced onion and a handful of parsley and chopped-up carrot. ☐ Bring to the boil and simmer for 40 minutes. ☐ Strain. ☐ Add 8oz of the stock to the drained raisin wine and bring to the simmer. ☐ Squeeze in the lemon juice and a couple of dashes of Worcester sauce. ☐ Check the seasoning and add the pheasant and raisin to heat through. ☐ Finally, incorporate double cream. ☐ Serve on a bed of rice with mushrooms together with a lettuce and orange salad.

Chicken in a Nightshirt

There is no difference in quality between a frozen and a fresh chicken, unless the one be battery reared and the other free-range and then the difference is infinite. Always roast a chicken breast-side down, after first depositing a 2 oz lump of butter, plus a bay leaf and half a chopped-up onion inside the cavity. Smear the carcase with more butter, plus seasoning. If cooking by electricity, slop in the pan 10 fl oz of stock or wine. For the last 20 minutes cook breast-side up and then baste every five minutes. As a variation, put in the cavity a sprig of tarragon, sage or fresh thyme. A combination of celery and cream cheese is surprisingly refreshing and on a warm day serve *Poulet-en-chemise*.

5 lb roasting chicken
2 Tbs olive oil
2 oz butter
24 shallots
1½ oz flour
6 juniper berries
1 bouquet garni
1 small tin pimentoes
8 oz button mushrooms
2 oz butter
1 Tbs lemon juice
1 orange
10 fl oz double cream
3 egg yolks
5 fl oz double cream
5 fl oz dry white wine
1 Tbs Curaçao

Cut chicken into 8 serving pieces and sauté gently in olive oil and butter until golden. Add peeled shallots (or very small onions) and shake around until glistening. □ Stir in flour. □ Add water to cover, season, add juniper berries, bouquet garni and pimentoes, drained and sliced. □ Cook softly for 1½ hours when the chicken should be tender. □ Remove the chicken, shallots and pimentoes to a large serving dish. □ Strain the stock. □ Sauté button mushrooms in butter and lemon juice. Drain, add to the chicken and sprinkle with grated orange rind. □ Now whisk egg yolks with orange juice and double cream until thick. □ Strain the stock and bring to the boil. □ Add a little of the hot stock to the cream and whisk furiously. □ Now add the rest of the stock gradually, whisking until absorbed. □ Pour the sauce into a saucepan and stir over gentle heat until it begins to thicken. □ Cool. □ Now whisk in cream and white wine plus Curaçao and combine with the chicken. □ Decorate with pimento strips, black olives and more grated orange peel. □ Serve with an orange and chicory salad and hot French bread and creamy butter.

Veal and Ham Pie

When I first arrived in London I was lucky to be taken under the wing of Hawkie (Miss Hawkins) who was nanny at the house in which I had taken rooms. When the doctor owners were on duty and the children asleep, Hawkie would share with me her supper of homely things — bobboti, sweetbreads in a cream sauce, tongue in a chutney sauce and, my favourite, veal and ham pie. It was delicious, especially since during my first weeks in the capital I had had a surfeit of its counterfeit in pubs. Here is Hawkie's farmhouse version of veal and ham pie which I remember describing as 'fantastic'. I made it yesterday and the guests echoed my comment from long ago — it is as good hot as cold.

2 lb pie veal
1 shin bone
Stock
2 bay leaves
Bouquet garni
1 level Tbs parsley
6 black peppercorns
1 lb cooked gammon
3 hard-boiled eggs
1½-2 pt stock
8 oz flaky pastry
1 egg
Lemon
1 tsp olive oil
½ tsp salt

Place pie veal and shin bone in a large pan, and cover with stock. □ Add bay leaves, bouquet garni, chopped parsley and peppercorns. □ Bring to the boil, cover the pan with a lid and simmer gently for 2 hours. □ Allow to cool slightly, then remove the meat from the liquid, cut into small pieces and remove any pieces of fat. □ Strain the liquid, season to taste with salt and pepper and set it aside. □ Cut piece of cooked gammon into narrow strips and mix with the veal. □ Shell hardboiled eggs, place them in the centre of a two-pint pie dish and pack the veal and gammon around them. □ Grate rind from lemon and sprinkle it over the top. □ Pour stock over the pie filling to just cover it. □ Roll out flaky pastry and cover the pie, with a slit in the centre. □ Beat egg, mix it with olive oil and salt and brush over the pastry. □ Bake the pie for 10 minutes in the centre of an oven preheated to 450 deg.F. (Gas Mark 8). □ Reduce the heat to 400 deg.F. (Gas Mark 6) and bake for a further 20 minutes or until the pastry is golden brown.

Rabbit Pie

Mother was very keen on food as part of a seduction technique. 'All men,' she said, 'are little boys at heart: they are most relaxed recollecting childhood suppers that sent them to bed to dream of rainbowland.' So she would invite the current favourite home and offer him boyhood food — rabbit pie served with recollections of chestnuts roasted in an open fire. I have altered her recipe to make a cold luncheon or picnic dish.

2½ lb rabbit
1 onion
1 carrot
1 bouquet garni
3 oz butter
3 oz flour
¾ lb shortcrust pastry
8 oz pâté
8 oz sliced pimento
1 egg

Joint rabbit (blanch if wild) and place in a pan, with cut up onion and carrot and bouquet garni. □ Season and cover with 1½in water. □ Simmer until tender (1 hour). □ Strain stock, cool and carve flesh. □ Make a roux from butter and flour and turn into thick sauce with rabbit stock. □ Roll out shortcrust pastry and line bottom and sides of 8½in spring-sided 2in deep cake tin. □ Dot base with pâté and sliced pimento. □ Cover pastry lid, seal and add egg glaze. □ Bake at 400 deg.F. (Gas Mark 6) for 1¼ hours. □ Cool before releasing spring.

Braised Oxtail

It is on those appetite-jading days of 80 degrees in the shade that the palate requires a stimulant: we should discard leaden mousse and flaccid salad and serve Spain's paella

and India's curry or our own braised oxtail.
The last dish is raised to Mediterranean
heights by a heady garnish of chopped
lemon peel and makes an extraordinarily
good summer luncheon.

2 oxtails
Seasoned flour
Dripping
2 onions
Bouquet garni
1 Tbs brown sugar
Juice of 1 orange
Pithless peel of 1 lemon
Red wine
Juice of 1 lemon
2 Tbs tomato paste
6 carrots
6 oz mushrooms
Noodles
Chopped parsley

Cut oxtails into pieces and roll in
seasoned flour. □ Fry in melted
dripping for 5 minutes together with
sliced onions. □ Add a bouquet garni,
sugar and orange juice plus the
pithless peel of lemon. □ Cover with
red wine, seal on lid and cook gently
on stove for 2 hours. □ Cool and skim
off fat. □ Add lemon juice, tomato
paste and cut-up carrots. □ Bring to
simmering point, adjust seasoning and
cook in oven, preset to 275 deg.F.
(Gas Mark 1) for 2½ hours. □ Stir in
cut-up mushrooms 15 minutes before
the end. □ Serve on a bed of buttered
noodles and smother the meat with a
mixture of chopped lemon peel and
parsley.

Spring Lamb

The springtime I thought was for love — of lamb. Succulent and young and in Wales roasted in a shroud of caul (kidney fat).
Real spring lamb is in fact a distant relative of those we see frisking in the fields. It is an earlier generation born in December and fed on its mother's milk until ready for the table in March. The snow-white creatures that make us misty-eyed in February come on sale in April-May at about 10p a pound extra, their mother's milk diet supplemented by fodder, linseed and maize or groundnut oil cake. The bulk from the hills reach us in August to October. The run of English lamb we eat in the spring is from the hogget, the animal that was a baby a year or more earlier and which by the following year will have become mutton — seemingly cornered nowadays by the Asian population.

My favourite way of cooking supposed lamb, that would be better dressed as mutton, turns a pedestrian shoulder into a dish which has a touch of Eastern promise.

1 shoulder of lamb
1 clove garlic
1 Tbs curry powder
3 Tbs honey
Salt
Pepper
Rice
Raisins
Fried nibbed almonds

Incise shoulder of lamb and slip in slivers of garlic. ☐ Rub the joint all over with a mixture of curry powder, honey, salt and pepper. ☐ Slow roast at 25 minutes to the pound in an oven preheated to 350 deg.F. (Gas Mark 4), in a tin which contains an inch of stock. ☐ Serve on a bed of rice into which raisins and fried nibbed almonds have been stirred.

Crown Roast with Cranberries

I've not known many Australians who can cook, which is surprising. I should have thought the younger generation would have learnt the rudiments, if only as self-defence against that *haute* of Australia's *haute cuisine* — well-grilled steaks with a fried egg on top. Recently an Australian friend returned home (he must remain anonymous, as they're vicious over there). This friend can cook quite well and is also a dab hand with a dry Martini, so you can see that his walkabout days are over. One night at dinner he served crown roast to the assembled guests, who included the literature editor of the Arts Council, Charles Osborne, the well known author and poet Julian Mitchell, and me. It was delicious, the centre being filled with highly seasoned blanched cauliflower which for the last half hour of cooking had absorbed the juice from the roast. The meal inspired me to experiment with fillings for a crown roast, and the one I like best has cranberries as its base.

1 crown roast
½ lb cranberries
1 oz caster sugar
¼ pt chicken stock
2 oz butter
1 onion
1 clove garlic
¼ lb mushrooms
½ lb minced belly pork
4 level Tbs parsley
1½ level tsp thyme
4 oz white breadcrumbs
1 Tbs redcurrant jelly
1 egg

For the stuffing put cranberries, caster sugar and chicken stock in a saucepan to cover the fruit. □ Bring to the boil and cook until they burst and the liquid has reduced to a thick sauce. □ Melt butter in a pan and fry chopped onion until soft but not coloured. □ Add peeled and crushed garlic clove and cook for 1 minute. □ Add chopped mushrooms, turning until they are lightly coloured. □ In a bowl combine the cranberries and the onion and mushroom mixture with minced belly pork. □ Mix in chopped parsley, ground thyme, fresh breadcrumbs and redcurrant jelly. □ Beat egg lightly and use to bind the stuffing. □ Season. □ Spoon the stuffing into the hollow crown. □ Roast on a shelf low in a preheated oven at 375 deg.F. (Gas Mark 5) for 10 minutes. □ Reduce the heat to 350 deg.F. (Gas Mark 4) and continue roasting for 1½ hours.

Kidneys in a Storm

Occasionally the weather is the one drawback of living in the country, especially when that means East Anglia. Not the showers or arrogant clouds, but deluges and winds that push over trees a couple of centuries old. Pylons topple spectacularly. They did in our neighbourhood when I was offering the first welcoming glass of Chambéry prior to a dinner party for seven. No electricity but, remembering my Boy Scout training, I hid the wild duck that was to have been served and out came the Calor twin-burner. With a willing slave holding a torch I cooked and proudly presented dinner. Even the electric light eventually came on again to brighten the applause which greeted the main course.

2 lamb kidneys (per person)
Black pepper
2 oz unsalted butter
Claret glass dry white wine
8 fl oz double cream
1 Tbs Dijon mustard
6 dashes of Worcester sauce
Salt
Pepper
Juice of 1 lemon
Patna rice
Mushrooms
Blanched peas
Green salad

Allow two lamb kidneys per person and slice each one in half. Cut out the core, then cut into ⅛in slices, grinding black pepper over the cut surfaces.
□ Melt butter in a pan and heat until it is beyond the frothy stage. □ Throw in the kidney slices and keep turning with a wooden spoon until they turn colour. □ Remove immediately from the heat and continue cooking until the blood runs (on gas with barely a glimmer of a flame and with electricity on a separate plate with a minimum of heat). □ Remove the kidneys and keep warm. □ Siphon off all but a scant tablespoon of butter and pour dry white wine into the pan (back on intense heat). □ Stir into this all the residue in the pan. □ Now add double cream, Dijon mustard, Worcester sauce, salt, pepper and lemon juice.
□ Cook for a minute or two until all is amalgamated. □ Serve the kidneys surrounded by Patna rice which has been boiled and then stirred in butter with chopped-up mushrooms and blanched peas. □ Pour the sauce over the kidneys and serve with a green salad.

Fidget Pie

My first doubt — that God took seven days to create the world and spent the rest of eternity fashioning the English to populate it — came when I went to my first point-to-point. At the 'off' the breed exhibited a fanaticism that culled memories of a gladiatorial arena; food and drink (but not dogs) took second place to young Felicity's success in the maiden race. She destroyed the field and, with stirrups akimbo, squeezed Bluebottle, a 16-hand bay across the finishing line — her thighs having the same effect as finger and thumb on a toothpaste tube. I avowed to avoid the English at their games. But in a Cotswold village I learned that their food was not the joke that foreigners projected. We had an Austrian cook, who had found refuge with us from the Nazis in 1933; to acknowledge her debt to her English hosts she recreated their dishes with devotion. A favourite simple luncheon dish was Fidget Pie.

1 lb potatoes
1 lb apples
½ lb diced green bacon
Brown sugar
½ pt stock
Seasoning
4 oz shortcrust pastry
1 egg

Arrange successive layers of sliced potatoes, apples and diced green bacon in a deep pie dish. □ Sprinkle a little brown sugar on the apples, cover with stock, season, and then top with shortcrust pastry. □ Egg glaze and bake at 400 deg.F. (Gas Mark 6) for 30 minutes and then for a further 10 minutes at 310 deg.F. (Gas Mark 2).

Pork

I have now contrived a series of dishes which, when served at luncheon, convince my city friends that life in the country is really the height of sophistication, not just a matter of avoiding cowpats and corrugated sheds.

Marinade

Hand of pork
½ pt white wine
4 Tbs wine vinegar
2 Tbs olive oil
2 cloves garlic
6 juniper berries
1 tsp peppercorns
4 bay leaves
1 tsp salt
1 Tbs brown sugar
½ tsp cinnamon

Stuffing

3 oz mixed dried fruits
4 oz white breadcrumbs
3 oz lean green bacon
1 tsp chopped chives
1 tsp chopped parsley
1 tsp chopped tarragon
Grated rind of 1 orange
1 small onion
1 clove garlic
3 oz butter
1 egg
Seasoning
Olive oil
Chicken stock

Get your butcher to bone a hand of
pork; remove the rind in one piece
and score it. ☐ Marinate (optional) the
cushion-shaped joint for 2 days in the
refrigerator, turning three times daily,
in white wine, wine vinegar, olive oil,
garlic, juniper berries (crushed),
peppercorns, bay leaves and salt.
☐ Drain and dry.

Make a stuffing by combining mixed
dried fruit, including peel, fresh
breadcrumbs, diced bacon, freshly
chopped chives, parsley, tarragon,
grated orange rind, grated onion,
garlic, melted butter, egg and
seasoning. ☐ Stuff and sew up joint.
☐ Place in roasting tin with rind,
rubbed with olive oil and salt, on top.
☐ Cover base of pan with ½in hot
chicken stock and roast at 400 deg.F.
(Gas Mark 6) for 15 minutes.
☐ Thereafter at 325 deg.F. (Gas Mark
2) for 45 minutes to the pound. Baste
every 30 minutes. ☐ Serve hot or cold
with new potatoes boiled and turned
over heat for 5 minutes in butter with
brown sugar and cinnamon.

Chicken Pie

One of the nicest things about this column is the letters I receive. The biggest flow came when 2 instead of 12 ounces of butter was quoted for Grandmama's Christmas Cake recipe. The switchboard was overwhelmed and cyclostyled replies had to be sent to the 500 or so who wrote in. One lady wrote me paeans of praise ending a leaf with a cry for help with a buffet party she was organising. On turning over the page I learned the buffet was for 400 people. I recommended her to stock five loaves and three little fishes. I also gave her this recipe for Chicken Pie, invaluable at buffets and picnics. To serve 12.

> **5 lb chicken**
> **12 shallots**
> **2 carrots**
> **1 heart of celery**
> **Bouquet garni**
> **Dry white wine**
> **Seasoning cube**
> **3 oz unsalted butter**
> **3 oz flour**
> **Shortcrust pastry**
> **9 lb liver pâté**
> **12 black olives, sliced**
> **8 oz tin pimentoes, sliced**
> **Salt**
> **Olive oil**

Joint the chicken and place in a saucepan with shallots, carrots, celery and bouquet garni. □ Cover with a mixture of half water and half dry white wine and a seasoning cube. □ Bring to the boil and simmer for 1 hour. □ Cool, skin the chicken and carve into slices. □ Melt butter in saucepan and make a roux with flour. □ Add the drained liquor from the chicken to make a thick sauce. □ Stir in carved chicken and cool. □ Line an 8½in spring-sided, plain-bottomed cake tin with shortcrust pastry bringing it up over the edge. □ Dot the base with knobs of liver pâté, pour in the chicken mixture into which has been stirred olives, and on top lay the drained contents of a tin of pimentoes. □ Cover with the remainder of the shortcrust pastry, sealing the edges. □ Decorate with pastry leaves, slit the steam hole and glaze with egg beaten with salt and olive oil. □ Bake at 400 deg.F. (Gas Mark 6) for 1½ hours. Protect top with foil when golden. □ Cool on rack and only release sides of tin when quite cold.

Two Winter Beef Dishes

It was in the early seventies that I created my version of *Carbonnade à la Flamande* and I have made it the same way ever since with expensive lean blade of beef — that is, until yesterday. My butcher, Ray, sold me some particularly good shin of beef. At home I had plenty of onions. So I made it with the cheaper shin, trimming away its excess fat and, with it, necessarily some of the meat. With the trimmings I intended to make a good beef stock. But its cooked flavour was so reminiscent of braised oxtail that from it I made a pudding which will defy the onslaught of even the worst weather.

Carbonnade
4 lb shin of beef
4 oz beef dripping
1 Tbs olive oil
2 lb onions
4 cloves garlic
2 level Tbs plain flour
1 level Tbs brown sugar
½ pt beef stock
¾ pt real old ale/barley wine/brown ale
1 Tbs wine vinegar
Juice of 1 lemon
1 bouquet garni
2 bay leaves
Garlic crust
1 French loaf
½ lb butter
4 cloves garlic

Trim the fat away from shin of beef and cut the lean meat in ¼in thick slices. ☐ Melt beef dripping in a sauté pan along with olive oil. In this quickly brown the beef. ☐ Slice onions finely and cook gently in the fat left in the pan until straw-coloured. ☐ Crush and mix in cloves of garlic. ☐ Layer the onions and the beef in a deep casserole. ☐ Mix into the juices left in the sauté pan plain flour and brown sugar until it makes a roux. ☐ Into this gradually stir beef stock and bring to the boil while stirring. ☐ Add draught old real ale or else bottled barley wine or just brown ale, plus wine vinegar and lemon juice. ☐ Simmer and season. ☐ Put in the casserole with a tight fitting lid and cook overnight at 250 deg.F. (Gas Mark ½).

(For the beef pudding, place the trimmings from the shin in another tight-lidded casserole, throw in a bouquet garni and bay leaves, cover with water and cook alongside the *Carbonnade*).

When serving, reheat and top with a garlic crust — stir 4 crushed cloves of garlic in ½lb butter as it melts. ☐ Cut a French stick loaf in ½in thick slices and put into the pan until the butter is absorbed. ☐ Cook the *Carbonnade* lidless, but bread-masked, at 325 deg.F. (Gas Mark 3) for 30 minutes.

Beef Pudding
Fat scraps of shin
¼ lb chopped mushrooms
4 oz chopped carrots
8 oz suet crust
Juice and rind of 1 lemon
Seasoning

Reheat the scraps cooked overnight in the casserole and stir into the meat chopped mushrooms, chopped carrot and lemon juice. ☐ Check seasoning and cool. ☐ Make a conventional suet crust but to it add the grated rind and juice of a lemon. ☐ Line a pudding basin with the pastry and spoon in the beef mixture (add a little more stock if needed). ☐ Seal with a pastry lid then cover with buttered greaseproof paper, putting on a pudding cloth and tie well. ☐ Lower on to some skewers placed in a pan of boiling water and boil for 3 hours. ☐ Both serve 6-8.

VEGETABLES & SALADS

Leeks with Rice

A year or so back I spent the winter working on a national cookery yearbook which has already sold nearly a million copies. I was determined to be original, and concocted combinations of which Dumas (he has written a cookery book, too) would have been proud. Unfortunately when reading other cookbooks (which I devour with the avidity an Agatha Christie fan has for her thrillers) I found that somebody had always been there first: nothing, it appeared, was new. My ego deflated day by day, until only my recipe for leeks-with-rice remained unchallenged (and what is the betting that some Anghared, in the hinterland of Wales, will write and tell me the day, and occasion, when she concocted the dish for her son Dafydd when he returned from altering the English sign posts to Welsh?).

2 lb leeks
3 oz melted butter
6 oz Patna rice
½ lemon
⅛ tsp curry powder
Black pepper
Seasoning

Remove the coarse outer leaves, roots and tops from leeks and wash aggressively. □ Slice the leeks in thick rounds, drop into a saucepan of boiling salted water for 5 minutes. □ Drain thoroughly and sauté in a pan with melted butter. □ Meanwhile boil Patna rice in salted water, with lemon, for 12 minutes. □ Wash the rice under hot running water and when clean and dry add to the leeks, turning the two together over heat. □ Add curry powder, a generous grinding of black pepper and serve with any casserole dish with which potatoes would be anathema — goulash, carbonnade, oxtail, et al.

Red Cabbage

It was in the kitchens of Le Français at Brighton that I learned a new way with red cabbage. Overlording the restaurant is the effervescent Yves Botasso; he not only pirouettes customers into accepting his standards front of house, but uses his ebullience backstage in the immaculate kitchens to gain an efficiency from a motley collection of assistants. 'Look,' he said, 'I asked for a vegetable chef and they sent me a fool, who's mother wouldn't trust 'im to slice potatoes for Lancashire 'otpot.' He buys the best but even he acknowledges the supremacy of the chef. Unconcerned by Botasso's Gallic showmanship he coolly carried on blanching batches of vegetables

to chill and finish for serving that evening.
With just a shrug to register a new crisis he
deposited ducks in ovens at 500 deg.F. to
cook for 30 minutes only, later to be
carved and cooked through in a
champagne sauce. I learned a lot that day
and the memories lived on when tasting
the quail pâté that the overwhelming M.
Botasso pressed on me, and through
experimenting with the tins of green
peppercorns that he insisted I try. One trick
that has stood me in good stead was
Botasso's way with red cabbage.

1 red cabbage
Wine vinegar
Salt
Pepper
Coriander seeds

None of the long cooking with apple
and fruit — just a freshly cut cabbage
finely shredded and poached for 5
minutes in a little wine vinegar to
which has been added salt and pepper
and some coriander seeds. ☐ Brightly
coloured and crisp it was served cold.
☐ I serve it hot with pork chops, lamb
chops and even with goulash. It is
simply delicious.

Pineapple, Walnut and Shrimp Salad

A fruit (botanically
speaking) is the ripened
ovary of a plant enclosing
its seed or seeds. This
definition just about encompasses

everything from a poppy to a pea. For this week's recipe I shall think in terms of those fruits whose ripened ovaries are sweet and succulent or pulpy — and hope it does not spoil your pleasure of an apple (or pineapple) to know that it is just a sweet old ovary prevented from propagating by your nibbling.

Salad
1 pineapple
Juice of 1 lemon
2 pickled walnuts
4 oz shrimps

Dressing
4 Tbs cream
Juice of 1 lemon
Touch of cayenne pepper
1 dsp tomato ketchup
Worcester sauce
Angelica 'leaves'

Cut pineapple into 6 wedges.
☐ Carefully cut and throw away the core. Pare out the fruit flesh and cut into small pieces, which you drop into a basin and sprinkle with the lemon juice. ☐ Finely cut pickled walnuts and add to the pineapple along with shrimps. ☐ Make a dressing by combining whipped cream, lemon juice, a touch of cayenne pepper, tomato ketchup and a suspicion of Worcester sauce. ☐ Mix lightly. ☐ Pile up the pineapple mixture into the wedges of skin and spoon the sauce over. ☐ Decorate with angelica 'leaves' and serve either as a first course or as a salad to accompany lamb chops or steak.

Stewed Lilies

My mother was always over-dramatic and when she served us this dish she could not simply give it a name from her Welsh origins (for the leek shares with the daffodil the honour of being the national emblem of Wales, its green and white colouring being emblazoned in Henry Tudor's coat-of-arms), but she had to display her horticultural prowess as well; and since the leek is a member of the lily family that was what she called it. The dish's quality surpassed the oddness of its nomenclature. Perhaps the leek needs a dramatic push, for it is a somewhat neglected vegetable often being relegated to just adding flavours to stews. But blanched, sliced and turned in butter with heavily black-peppered boiled rice it makes a perfect accompaniment to casseroled dishes; cooked in stock, then sliced and made into a pie with a bit of bacon and cream and egg filling, it creates a simple luncheon dish, or first course for dinner. It is also practically the only vegetable which does not suffer from being frozen without first being blanched. What more could one ask?

3 lb leeks
Salt
Juice of 1 lemon

Sauce
1 tsp Dijon mustard
Black pepper
1 tsp chopped parsley
1 dsp chopped shallot
1 Tbs white wine vinegar
5 Tbs olive oil

You must choose leeks that are young and no thicker than a plump stick of asparagus; these will average about 6-7 a pound. Thoroughly clean by cutting off the root and peeling away the outer skin. Also cut off the tough green leaves at the top; that is where the dirt really hides. □ Prise open each leek and wash under a strongly running tap to get rid of every vestige of grit. □ When clean, plunge them into a saucepan of boiling water, well-seasoned with salt and lemon juice. □ Simmer for 8 minutes or until tender. □ Drain thoroughly, pressing out the excess water gently with your fingers. □ When they are quite cold, place them in a gratin dish and cover with the following sauce.

Put in a largish bowl Dijon mustard, good grating of black pepper, finely chopped parsley and chopped shallot. □ Now mix in wine vinegar and olive oil, a teaspoon at a time. □ Add a sprinkle of salt if needed. □ The leeks should remain in this sauce for at least 3 hours before serving as a first course.

Spinach Catalan

I have eaten *paella* on the lush lawns of a grand house in Seville and savoured a meticulously planned meal in one of the government-sponsored luxurious *parador* hotels. Everything was well done. But I am still not as enthusiastic about Spanish mainland cuisine as that which I enjoyed on Minorca, one of the Balearic Islands not as yet swamped by tourists. On Minorca's northern seaboard is Manola, one of the world's best fish restaurants nestling in the film-set harbour of Cuidadela. To the south east, in the harbour of Mahon, is another restaurant, The Rocamar, whose owner, Antonio Borras, serves superb food in the summer and in the winter sings bass in Barcelona's Gran Teatro del Liceo. But one of the most interesting places I visited was a small farmhouse restaurant at Torret called Isla de los Porros. I appreciated its simplicity and they produced a first course which I enjoyed enough to ask for the recipe. But I could not drag it from them. So here is my version.

2 lb spinach
3 oz butter
1 clove garlic
Juice of 1 lemon
2 oz raisins
Black pepper
2 oz pinenuts

For four people, blanch well-washed spinach in a pan of salted water.
□ Drain and press out the liquid.
□ Melt butter in a pan; in it fry lightly a crushed clove of garlic and then allow the spinach to cook until tender in the butter. □ Add the lemon juice, raisins and copious black pepper.
□ Separately fry pinenuts until golden and turn in the spinach mixture.
□ Serve with toast fingers, dipped in butter in which a clove of garlic has been fried gently.

Game and Waldorf Salad

I cannot let the Glorious Twelfth go by without having a shot at game.

Grouse is in season from August 12 until December 10. There are several kinds, but the bird which really predominates is the Red or Scottish grouse. It is at perfection at the end of August; by late October it has grown a little too old for straight roasting and should then be relegated to the terrine, casserole or pie. A young grouse requires little hanging — just a few days. Roasted properly, its flesh should eat like pâté. The partridge appears in the gun sights on October 1 and gains its reprieve on February 1. The pheasant is in season from October 1 to January 31 (December 10 in Scotland). Here is an ideal salad to accompany these poor birds.

1 lb tart red dessert apples
2 Tbs lemon juice
1 level tsp caster sugar
1 Tbs mayonnaise
1 head of celery
2 oz walnuts
¼ pt mayonnaise
1 lettuce
Olive oil
1 crushed clove garlic

Wash and core dessert apples. □ Slice one apple finely and dice the others. □ Dip the apple slices in a dressing of lemon juice, caster sugar and mayonnaise, and set aside. □ Toss the diced apple in the dressing and let stand for 30 minutes. □ Add celery, finely chopped, and shelled chopped walnuts plus further mayonnaise. □ Line a serving bowl with lettuce leaves, wiped over with olive oil into which a clove of garlic has been crushed. □ Pile the mixed salad into the centre and circle with the apple slices.

Potato Dishes

The King Edward potato must move into the background for me. Red Desirée will soon be the champion. It is, in my opinion, so infinitely superior to the older variety. The demise of a long-time favourite, once so popular that

it was involved in dubious music-hall
'royal' jokes, is a little sad, but I now use
the ubiquitous Red Desirée for boiling,
frying, baking and roasting. I still keep a
supply of Golden Wonder for sauté
potatoes; they are champions in that field.

2 lb Red Desirée Potatoes
Salt
Pepper
1 clove garlic
2 oz unsalted butter
½ pt double cream

Slice Red Desirées ⅛in thick and stand
in salted water for 10 minutes.
□ Meanwhile rub round a gratin dish
with a clove of garlic and then butter
thickly. □ Layer the potatoes in the
dish, seasoning at each layer. □ Dot
with butter and pour over double
cream and bake at 375 deg.F. (Gas
Mark 5) for 40 minutes.

or
2 lb potatoes
2 oz butter
3 Tbs double cream
1 Tbs dark bitter marmalade
1 egg
Toasted breadcrumbs

Force barely boiled potatoes through a
sieve, mash over heat with butter and
double cream and stir in marmalade.
□ Form into croquettes, roll through
beaten egg, then fine toasted
breadcrumbs — and repeat.
□ Refrigerate for 30 minutes. □ Deep
fry at 390 deg.F. (Gas Mark 6) for 3
minutes.

or
6 large potatoes
2 oz unsalted butter
4 fl oz double cream
1 clove garlic
3 eggs

Wash and dry potatoes, prick lightly
with a fork and bake for 1½ hours, or
until tender, on the middle shelf of an
oven preheated to 400 deg.F. (Gas
Mark 6). □ Cut a lid lengthways off the
baked potatoes, scoop the flesh out
into a bowl and mix in with it unsalted
melted butter, double cream and
crushed garlic clove. □ Stir egg yolks
into the mixture. □ Beat the egg
whites stiffly and combine with the
potato. □ Pile this soufflé mixture
back into the hollow potato skins, and
bake for 15 minutes, when the soufflés
will be well risen.

Cabbage Quiche

I had twin aunts called
Abigail Cattura and
Vashti Tabitha. They
were my father's sisters
and were condemned as
undesirables by Mother
. . . so I saw very little of them. But
Grandmama insisted I visit them once a
year. This I did at the boarding school they
ran in the Cotswolds. The visits were
pleasant. The vicar always came in for
sherry on Sunday — for me, a rare
experience (back home our household was
regarded by the clergy as the eighth deadly

sin). I was glad, though, when the visit was over — a halitosis of cabbage odour enveloped the school. It was revolting. It was years before I became a cabbage-lover and this week's recipe has been developed to convert cabbage-haters to the delight of the vegetable.

Shortcrust pastry
6 oz plain flour
3½ oz butter
1 egg
Salt

Filling
Small cabbage
White wine
Nutmeg
6 peppercorns
½ pt double cream
3 eggs
Seasoning

Make a rich shortcrust pastry from plain flour, butter, salt and an egg. □ Rest in fridge. □ Finely shred cabbage, poach for 5 minutes in white wine with salt and peppercorns (substitute wine vinegar if no oddment of wine available). □ Drain until cool. □ Line an 8in flan ring with the pastry, spread in cabbage, sprinkle with a lavish sprinkling of nutmeg. □ Beat together double cream, eggs and seasoning. □ Pour over cabbage. □ Place in oven at 425 deg.F. (Gas Mark 7) for 10 minutes and then for 20 minutes at 350 deg.F. (Gas Mark 4). □ Serve as a vegetable with grilled or roasted meats.

Parsnips Molly Parkin

Parsnips are thought to have an aphrodisiac quality and that, may make them more attractive than any words of mine about cooking the root. But beware of seducing the loved one with a glass or two of parsnip wine; I can vouch for its laxative effect.

2 lb parsnips
1 lb tomatoes
5 Tbs oil
3 oz butter
3 level Tbs soft brown sugar
Salt, black pepper
6 oz Gruyère cheese
½ pt single or double cream
4 Tbs white breadcrumbs

Peel and slice the parsnips thinly, discarding any hard central cores.
□ Skin the tomatoes, and cut the flesh into slices. □ Heat the oil in a pan and lightly fry the parsnips for 4 minutes.
□ Grease a 2pt casserole dish with half the butter, and place a layer cf parsnips over the base. □ Sprinkle with a little sugar, salt, freshly ground pepper and add a little cream, before covering with a layer of tomatoes. □ Spread a little more cream and cheese over the tomatoes and repeat these layers until all the ingredients are used up, finishing off with cream and cheese. □ Top with the breadcrumbs and dot with the remaining butter. □ Cook the parsnip casserole for 40 minutes in an oven pre-heated to 325 deg.F (Gas Mark 3).

PUDDINGS

Christmas Pudding

Christmas at home was never dull; my opera singer mother always returned in the nick of time to take charge of the festivities. She was magnificent with the detail — like organising a nativity play as colossal as *Aida* — but usually managed to forget something obvious such as the turkey. You can imagine the chagrin a household felt, sitting down to a tin of honey-cured ham tarted-up with chestnut stuffing, bacon rolls and chipolata sausages. Luckily Grandmama made the puddings and they were always superb — she used butter instead of suet in their making.

4 oz flour
½ level tsp nutmeg, cinnamon, mixed spice
1 level tsp salt
4 oz almonds
8 oz breadcrumbs
1 lb stoned raisins
2 oz mixed peel
8 oz currants
8 oz sultanas
12 oz unsalted butter
4 oz soft brown sugar
6 eggs
4 Tbs brandy
8 fl oz milk

Sieve together flour, nutmeg, cinnamon, mixed spice, salt, 2oz ground almonds, and fresh breadcrumbs. □ Then mix in stoned raisins, mixed peel, almonds (all chopped) currants and sultanas. □ Separately beat together until light and fluffy unsalted butter and soft brown sugar. □ Now beat into the butter, eggs — thoroughly and one at a time. □ Combine with dry ingredients then add brandy and as much as you need of milk to give a soft dropping consistency. □ This mixture makes two 2½lb puddings. □ Divide between two basins, cover each with greaseproof, then with a cloth, and steam for 6 hours. □ Remove cloth and greaseproof and re-cover with fresh when cool. □ On Christmas Day keep to the boil for 4 hours. □ Serve on a tray festooned with a holly garland and set the pudding ablaze with brandy.

Pear Flan

There is a generosity about the contented exiled Briton which I find enviable: he never bores by whining for home, but concentrates on making your stay in his adopted country happy. Among the best of this breed is a man called Ian McGill. He has lived in Paris for, say, 20 years, writes a food column and demonstrably enjoys himself. He took me for dinner a whiplash off the amazing Rue St. Denis at Chez Benoit, 'the best place to eat in Paris outside the Laserre/Tour d'Argent stratum,' he said. Afterwards we had drinks at Lipp's — the Cabinet eats there on Wednesday, and B.B., it is said, has paraded the block for one-and-a-half hours waiting for a downstairs table. (Even the King and Queen of Greece could not set a new fashion for eating upstairs at night). The pudding that night was *Tarte au Poire* — with it there must always be a taste of almonds, and for me a taste of France.

Rich shortcrust pastry
5 dessert pears
Sugar syrup
8 oz water
4 oz butter
4 oz caster sugar
2 eggs
Juice of 1 lemon
4 oz ground almonds

Line a flan with rich shortcrust pastry, peel, core and halve pears and poach for 5 minutes in sugar syrup and with the pithless peel of half a lemon. □ Spread over the flan base an almond paste (butter, creamed with caster sugar, eggs beaten-in singly, lemon juice and ground almonds). □ Arrange the pears in cartwheel fashion and bake at 425 deg.F. (Gas Mark 7) for 10 minutes and at 350 deg.F. (Gas Mark 4) for a further 20 minutes. □ Serve warm.

Champagne Charlie

This pudding is for all those mothers who have a favourite son called Charles; let them use it only on ultra-important occasions such as a 21st birthday party or wedding celebration. It was devised to mark the first visit to my 'new' home in Suffolk of a family friend, familiarly called Charlie. For dinner on that night I devised dishes-with-a-difference and named them after the guests. We began with *Soup Julie*, scorzonera-based. Then followed slices of smoked salmon wrapped around smoked cods roe (pounded into a mousse with lemon juice and cream — then sprinkled with caviar), *Papillotes de saumon fumé van Til*. The main course was the familiar, *Filet de boeuf en croûte* but appended '*à la Lili*', for she bought me a tin of four truffles. But the *pièce de résistance* was the dish named after the guest-of-honour, *Champagne Charlie*. 'Charlie' needs genuine champagne, it will tingle on the tongue as you take the first frozen spoonful: you will be shown up if you substitute an inferior sparkling wine.

6 oz caster sugar
¼ pt water
3 oranges
3 lemons
1 pt chilled champagne
1 pt double cream
2 Tbs brandy
6 ratafia biscuits
1 dsp brandy (each glass)
Ice cream
1 tsp brandy (each glass)

Put caster sugar in a pan with water. Boil rapidly for 6 minutes to make a syrup. □ Grate into it the rind of an orange and add the juice of 2 oranges and lemons. □ Cool. □ Stir in chilled champagne. □ Freeze for 1½-2 hours, until frozen round the edges. □ Now whip until smooth. □ Fold in whipped double cream and brandy. □ Freeze for about 3 hours. □ Soak ratafia biscuits in each champagne glass with brandy. □ Scoop the ice cream into the glasses, pour a teaspoon of brandy over each portion. □ Hang a spiral of lemon peel from each glass and serve with Taittinger Sec.

Strawberry and Peach Vacherin

Picnics on the beach fill me with horror. From the outset sand, children and dogs noisily defeat the tranquil purpose. But when I moved to Suffolk I found Dunwich. It has crumbling sandstone cliffs and miles of pebbles. It was here I served my first beach picnic on a sunny weekday in July, and magically I produced as pudding a towering edifice of meringue, *crème pâtissière*, cream, strawberries and peaches. It was so bizarre a scene in that isolated spot that it seemed like something more out of an Antonioni movie. The secret was the magnificent freezer boxes that keep food hot or cold for 12 hours.

Meringue
5 whites of 'shop' eggs
5 oz granulated sugar
5 oz caster sugar
Pinch of salt

Filling
1 lb mulled strawberries
10 fl oz double cream
Peaches

Make the meringue by beating together the egg whites with a pinch of salt until they mount to a foam; sprinkle on the granulated sugar and beat on until stiff. Fold in the caster sugar lightly. □ Pipe and spread on rice paper to form three circles, 8in, 5in and 4in diameter (on the smaller circle, pipe trails of meringue to form a collapsing stalagmite of decoration). □ Dry out in the oven at 265 deg.F. (Gas Mark 1) until faintly coloured (but it should be toffee-like in the middle). □ Make *crème pâtissière* as shown below and assemble. □ Spread *crème* on largest meringue, cover with ½lb strawberries, then a layer of lightly whipped double cream. □ Now put on the next meringue layer, more *crème*, more strawberries, plus thinly sliced peaches, more cream, then crown the lot with the meringue tiara. □ Chill and serve to a round of applause.

Crème Pâtissière
½ pt milk
3 egg yolks
4 oz caster sugar
1 vanilla pod

Place egg yolks, flour and sugar in a bowl and beat vigorously until smooth. ☐ Meanwhile heat milk and vanilla pod in a saucepan and bring slowly to just below boiling point. ☐ Pour milk on eggs and beat. ☐ Pour into double saucepan and cook slowly, stirring until custard thickens.

Eton Boater Pudding

Grandmama was determined that I should be educated. 'What can a boy learn,' she said to my mother, 'but bad habits, living out of a trunk on an operatic tour?' Eventually I was allowed to stay home with grandmum, and one of my first lessons was A Visit to The Theatre. 'We are going to the temperance hall that Emma Con's niece, the young Miss Bayliss, has made such a success. It is now known as The Old Vic, and we are going to see *Hamlet* by William Shakespeare.' Passers-by stared at the very tall old lady, wearing a hat that seemed a mass of pink chaffinches, talking in a well articulated but very loud voice seemingly to the world at large. At her feet scurried a small boy of six — me. Mercifully I cannot remember one bit of the performance.

Afterwards we ate at a little French restaurant that knew Grandmama well and we were escorted to a table with a pretty pink cloth. From lessons back home I ordered *Sole Véronique, Mousse à la Périgourdine* and strawberries. Strawberries I adored, dunked in grandmum's champagne or served with cream for breakfast; but this night they took on a new height in a dessert which grandmama declared to be the *Eton Boater Pudding* (which the menu announced as *Crème Waflen*). Afterwards I was sick, but beautifully so. Grandma had seen *Hedda Gabler* and had been much affected by it. Therefore anything unpleasant had to be done *beautifully*.

> 2 oz caster sugar
> Juice of 1 lemon
> 1 lb strawberries
> ½ lb ratafias
> Claret glass sherry/port/brandy
> Apricot jam
> 8 in sponge cake
> Wafer biscuits
> 1 pt double cream

Sprinkle caster sugar and the lemon juice over strawberries and ratafias, then pour over claret glass of sherry, port or brandy. □ Leave for 1 hour. □ Spread apricot jam over the sides of a sponge cake and afix wafer biscuits to form a wall: cement the joints with royal icing. □ Tie a wide ribbon around the biscuits. □ Whisk double cream, fold in the fruit and pour it over the sponge. □ Decorate the top with more fruit and ratafias.

Welsh Bread Pudding

I remember the last day of October as Ducking Apple Night. As children we had been taught that the apple is the most holy of fruit and that it would never cause us any harm; so it was considered natural that it should have a measure of magic about it. Blindfolded, we found our luck by 'ducking' for the apples in a tub of water. The one who caught the largest (in his teeth) gained the promise of the biggest fortune during the coming year. Before the ducking, we had had our fill of dark streets, lanterns and spooks. Now, damp from the tub, we looked forward to the best part of the evening, our treat, when we were given a slice of Welsh Bread Pudding warm from the oven. (It makes a good lunch pudding with thick cream).

8 oz stale bread
10 fl oz milk
2 oz candied peel
Grated rind of 1 orange
and 1 lemon
4 oz currants
2 oz sultanas
3 oz shredded beef suet
2 oz demerara sugar
2 level tsp mixed spice
1 egg
Nutmeg
Butter
Caster sugar

Cut and discard the crust from stale white bread and soak in milk for 20 minutes. □ Finely chop candied peel, add to the bread along with the grated rind of an orange and lemon, currants, sultanas, beef suet, demerara sugar and mixed spice. □ Blend well, then add a beaten egg. □ Stir all together. □ If necessary, add a dessertspoon of milk to give a 'dropping' consistency. □ Spoon into a well-greased 2 pt pie dish and grate over a little nutmeg. □ Bake at 350 deg. F. (Gas Mark 4) for about 2 hours, or until browned. □ Serve hot or cold, sprinkled with caster sugar.

John's Apple Flan

Tomorrow John gets married — at five o'clock in the afternoon. During the early summer his intended did a not-so-grand-tour of Italy, a last fling to mark the imminent transformation of Miss into Mrs. But John, eminently practical, insidiously asked me to the opera to hear Monsarrat Caballe in *Il Trovatore* and coaxed me into teaching him a few cooking tricks. The flan in question is good served as it is, but better when I have included a handful of mixed dried fruit along with the apple. That night there was no fruit and John commented 'If only you had said, I'd have made us toffee-apples instead'. Eureka! A new dish was born.

Shortcrust pastry
6 oz flour
3½ oz soft butter
Salt
1 dsp icing sugar
1 egg yolk

Filling
Slices of apple
5 fl oz double cream
1 whole egg
2 oz soft brown sugar
Demerara sugar

To flour add butter, a pinch of salt and icing sugar. With the tips of the fingers quickly mingle until crumbly — do not overrub. ☐ Now with a fork mix in beaten egg and then knead until smooth and shiny. ☐ Rest enclosed in a polythene bag in the refrigerator for 30 minutes. ☐ Roll out and line an 8in flan tin; where it tears, repair by using offcuts like putty. ☐ Fill the case with thick slices of apple, pour over double cream beaten with 1 whole egg and soft brown sugar. ☐ Bake for 10 minutes in an oven heated to 450 deg.F. (Gas Mark 8) then lower the heat to 400 deg.F. (Gas Mark 6) for a further 20 minutes. ☐ Remove the cooked flan from the oven and cover it with ⅛in thickness of demerara sugar, then protect the pastry edge with foil and put under a really fierce grill for a few minutes until the sugar turns to toffee. ☐ Let cool and serve warm with thick cream.

Raspberry Pudding

Wild Peter Langan
rocketed to fame
when he opened
Langan's Brasserie in
Stratton Street: his
face was splattered in most of the gossip
columns, along with his clientele from
Princess Anne down. Strangely, his
partner, Michael Caine, got his share of
publicity, too — with Peter's gift as an
outrageous storyteller I would not have
imagined anybody else getting a look-in.
Anyway, his is the only restaurant I have
entered for dinner at 8.30 in the evening
and left at 8.30 next morning — with him
still talking as he saw me out the door.
Food was our permanent topic of
conversation and his enthusiasm was
tremendous.

One day he told me of his earlier
experiences at the original Odins (his posh
new Odins is in Devonshire Street, and
still a delight to eat in). 'Money was a bit
scarce then,' he said, 'and this Charlie
came to the door and offered me a load of
raspberries, cheap. They were on the
menu in a flash, as a sorbet and as fresh
raspberries and cream. All went well until a
customer claimed they were "bubbling". I
told him it was the sugar and disappeared
into the kitchen. They were all over the
place — in the heat they'd started to
ferment. I thought to turn them into a drop
of the hard stuff, but discretion prevailed
and I threw them away.' At the time his
pudding list was a bit sparse so I gave him
this recipe for raspberry charlotte which I

acquired in Paris. Understandably, perhaps, it never appeared on his menu. But it is one of my favourite raspberry puddings.

1 lb sponge fingers
Curaçao
6 oz caster sugar
6 oz unsalted butter
6 oz ground almonds
5 fl oz Cointreau
1 lb raspberries
Juice of 1 lemon

Butter soufflé dish well enough to fix sponge fingers to its side. ☐ Line the bottom with them too — the sponge fingers first having been sprinkled copiously with Curaçao. ☐ Beat caster sugar, unsalted butter and ground almonds together until fluffy, then beat in 2 fluid ounces of Cointreau. ☐ Sprinkle more sponge fingers with more Cointreau (3 fluid ounces). ☐ Fill the soufflé dish with alternate layers of almond butter, soaked sponge fingers, and raspberries, finishing with a layer of sponge fingers. ☐ Weight and refrigerate overnight. ☐ Turn out and serve with a sauce made from raspberries passed through a sieve, to which has been added the juice of a lemon.

Banana and Apricot Flan Alberto

To my mind the owners of the best restaurants in the country have to show a combination of dedication, effort and charm. Such a dedicated professional runs the restaurant of the Viking Hotel in York. It is one of the Grand Metropolitan Group and although not quite bracketable with Claridge's, it has Alberto and he is worth all the flurry of Norsemen oars which trick out the walls. He has panache, style and perfectionism which I have never seen bettered (not even at The Savoy, where he was trained). The food at The Viking Hotel is on the whole all right, but Alberto will deftly supplement the menu with main course *flambé* dishes, or for pudding will flourish his copper pan to make even tinned peaches a delight. Inspired by his way with bananas I have devised a flan which is a winner.

Shortcrust Pastry
6 oz self-raising flour
1 level dsp icing sugar
3½ oz salted butter
Squeeze of lemon juice
1 egg

Filling
3 oz caster sugar
2 heaped tsp apricot preserve
2 fl oz Cointreau
3 fl oz double cream
5 bananas
3 fl oz brandy
Juice of 1 lemon

Make a sweet shortcrust pastry from flour, icing sugar, salted butter, lemon juice and 1 whole egg. ☐ Rest it in a polythene bag in the refrigerator for 30 minutes. ☐ Roll out and line an 8-9in flan ring with the pastry, roll the edge clean with your pin and check that nary a pinhole pierces the pastry. ☐ Rest it again in the refrigerator. ☐ Meanwhile boil together caster sugar with 4 fl oz water until it makes a thick but pourable syrup. In another pan, melt the apricot preserve with the lemon juice. ☐ Beat the syrup and melted apricot together until smooth and stir in Cointreau and double cream. ☐ Peel bananas and split lengthwise (sometimes there is a bitter ⅛in core that is best removed). ☐ Cut across in the short direction and arrange the bananas cut side down, Catherine wheel fashion, on to the base of the flan — it rarely works out neatly. ☐ Pour the syrup mixture over the bananas and place the flan in an oven preheated to 450 deg.F. (Gas Mark 7) and immediately turn the heat control down to 350 deg.F. (Gas Mark 3) and allow to cook for 30 minutes, when the pastry will be just shrinking away from the walls of the flan ring. ☐ Keep in a warm place, but do not attempt to transfer from the baking ring to the serving dish for a further 15 minutes. ☐ Take to the table with a pan containing heated brandy, pour over the flan *flambé* and douse the flame by squeezing the lemon juice over the top.

Thursday's Tarts

Thursday is the day I go out to eat or, if I eat at home, it is the day I declare that fruit and cheese will do. That is, until the impossible occurred: I had two children staying at my house. It was too late for me to leave for foreign parts. Besides, I thought of the damage they would have done had I not been there to threaten annihilation if they so much as breathed let alone moved. I confess to allowing them to play overlong in the garden, in the hope they might fall into the moat. They were there because their mother had an accident, and it seemed there was nowhere the children could go. I thought children liked savoury things until these two arrived — hence these two tarts, which turned out to be their favourites. Of the two, the butterscotch was preferred by my guests; I think because at first its appearance made them think it was to be the old familiar lemon meringue pie. But the toffee filling made it most decidedly a 'seconds' dish for them. Both recipes came from a mother of six (children, I mean!)

Butterscotch Flan
Sweet shortcrust pastry
3 eggs
10 oz soft brown sugar
2 oz flour
½ tsp vanilla essence
¼ pt rich milk
1 oz butter
3 oz granulated sugar

Line a 9in flan ring with shortcrust pastry, prick, cover with crumpled foil and bake blind at 325 deg.F. (Gas Mark 3) for 20 minutes, the last 5 minutes with foil removed. □ For the filling, beat yolks of 3 eggs and soft brown sugar together until fluffy. □ Beat in flour, vanilla essence and milk. □ Cook in the top of a double saucepan until thick. □ Stir in butter. □ Cool and pour into flan case. □ Beat together 3 egg whites until stiff and fold in granulated sugar. □ Spread this meringue on top of the butterscotch and bake at 300 deg.F. (Gas Mark 2) until tinged brown. □ Serve warm or cold.

Raspberry and Coconut Flan
Shortcrust pastry
3 Tbs raspberry jam
2 oz butter
2 oz caster sugar
1 egg
4 oz desiccated coconut
Pinch of salt

Line a 9in flan ring with shortcrust pastry and spread raspberry jam over the base. □ Cream together butter and caster sugar until fluffy. □ Gradually add beaten egg and dessicated coconut. □ Add salt. □ Spread over jam and bake at 350 deg.F. (Gas Mark 4) for 35 minutes. □ Serve hot.

Orange Gâteau

I have a friend who is very wise, very beautiful and occasionally eccentric. I am her mentor and she is the guru of our group. Her name is Elizabeth Smart and she wrote that classic *By Grand Central Station I Sat Down and Wept.* She gardens like a fanatic. One day, when she had her tiny tots of grandchildren at her feet, she heard the cry of the hunt; to her eternal guilt she felt doubt as to whether she should save the children or the newly-planted peonies from the thundering hooves. She cooks well, too. Often we search the countryside for plants and other things. One November day we found ourselves near Cambridge and we decided to eat at a well known local restaurant, Kims. The main course was pigeon. But for pudding we decided to move on and eat our own food, for she produced from a carrier bag an exquisite gâteau.

4 oz unsalted butter
8 oz caster sugar
2 eggs
8 oz plain flour
1 level tsp bicarbonate of soda
¼ pt milk
1 Tbs lemon juice
3 medium-sized oranges
6 oz chopped sultanas
4 oz chopped walnuts

Sauce
3 oz caster sugar
1 miniature Curaçao/Grand Marnier

111

Grease well a large angel cake tin (ring mould). ☐ Set your oven to 350 deg.F. (Gas Mark 4). ☐ Cream unsalted butter together with caster sugar until pale and fluffy and add beaten eggs, a little at a time. ☐ Sift plain flour and bicarbonate of soda and fold into the butter mixture, alternately with milk and lemon juice. ☐ Add the grated rinds of oranges, chopped sultanas and chopped walnuts. ☐ Turn into the prepared tin and bake for 1½ hours until well risen and firm to the touch. ☐ Leave the cake in the tin for 5 minutes before turning out on to a wire rack to cool slightly, then turn the cake upside down gently on to a cake rack.

For the sauce, dissolve caster sugar in the juice of the oranges and simmer on a low heat for 5 minutes. ☐ Add 1 miniature of Curaçao (or Grand Marnier) to the syrup. ☐ With a large plate underneath your cake, make incisions with a skewer all over its base and pour the syrup mixture over the cake gently until it has all been absorbed. Any that runs out, spoon over again. ☐ Now the cake can be served right way up.

Blackberry Pie

On September 30 I avoid eternal damnation by picking the last of the summer's blackberries from the hedgerow. A late summer often gives October the best berries, but by October 1

the Devil will have annexed the fruit as his
own by splattering it with spittle — or so 'tis
said. But come the new month — and if
the sun is still shining — then I shall risk his
worst and nick the best from beneath his
nose, cursing the thorns which prick (but
yet are supposed to have softened
Lucifer's fall when he was bounced out of
Heaven). The picking done, I race home to
make blackberry pie. Not blackberry and
apple . . . that I consider an abomination. I
add ground almonds to the pastry which
makes for a marvellous complementary
crust.

Shortcrust Pastry
4 oz flour
2 oz ground almonds
1 dsp icing sugar
3 oz butter
Water

Filling
1½ lb blackberries
1 orange
3 oz sugar
Cream

Make shortcrust pastry from flour,
ground almonds, icing sugar and
butter, together with enough water to
make a paste and let rest. □ Fill a deep
pie dish with berries and sprinkle over
the juice and rind of the orange and
the sugar. □ Cover with the crust.
□ Run a cold tap over the pastry and
sprinkle caster sugar copiously over
the wet surface. □ Place in an oven
preheated to 425 deg.F. (Gas Mark 6)
for 10 minutes, then reduce heat to
375 deg.F. (Gas Mark 5) for a further
25 minutes. □ Serve with cream.

Gooseberry Cream

Grandmama kept a series of exercise books, bound in marbled paper with a linen strip running up the spine. In these she copied out, in a beautifully formed hand, a mass of information and useful ideas. This recipe is from her book on Cookery for Festival and Fast Days.

2 lb gooseberries
Grated rind and juice of ½ lemon
Caster sugar
½ pt milk
¼ pt double cream
1 oz gelatine
¼ pt white wine
¾ pt milk
Double cream, icing sugar, cinnamon

Wash, drain and gently cook gooseberries in water until soft and broken. □ Press them through a sieve, add the grated rind and lemon juice and sweeten to taste with caster sugar. □ Return to pan and simmer for 5 minutes, stirring. □ Warm together milk and double cream and in this dissolve gelatine. □ Stir into the gooseberry mixture and pour into a wetted mould. □ Let stand in a cool place until next day. □ Make the junket from white wine and milk, and when it curdles around the spoon, pour it over gooseberries to set. □ When serving, pour over a little double cream (without disturbing the curd) and dust the top with icing sugar mixed with a little cinnamon.

CAKES & THINGS

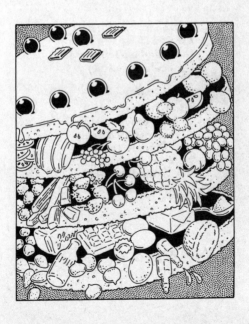

Mint Pastry

The northern cake shops still sell proper home-made cakes and pastries, the variety of which has disappeared in southern counties to be replaced mainly by Kunzle or Kipling. A few years ago I went to the wedding of my friend Jack Clements in Bradford. The reception was in his parents' house in Lidget Green, dominated by an enormous mill chimney around the rim of which, they announced proudly, a horse and cart could drive. At the reception there was a mint pastry so delicious it might even have rivalled my already quoted Welsh Bread Pudding in popularity (and that dish, dear readers, caused one family group to call me Uncle Denis).

Shortcrust Pastry
8 oz self-raising flour
1 rounded tsp icing sugar
4½ oz butter

Filling
3 oz currants
2 oz stoned raisins
1 oz candied peel
Chopped mint
2 oz brown sugar
Grated nutmeg
Granulated sugar

Make a shortcrust pastry by rubbing together flour, icing sugar and butter. Bind with a little water. □ Rest and roll out thickly and cut into rounds the size of a tea cup. □ On half of these rounds put a layer of currants, stoned raisins and peel chopped finely. □ Sprinkle with finely chopped mint and brown sugar. □ Dab with small knobs of butter and grate nutmeg over the top. □ Wet the edges of the pastry and cover with another round, pinching the edges together. □ Brush with water and sprinkle with granulated sugar. □ Bake at 375 deg.F. (Gas Mark 5) for 25-30 minutes.

Tea at Tannochbrae

I was visiting Barbara Mullen a few years back in the sitting-room of Arden house at the television studios for one of the *Dr. Finlay's Casebook* episodes, 'I am not a dedicated cook,' said Miss Mullen, as we took tea, 'and had you not brought all these lovely cakes then I think we would have had to make do with a cup of canteen tea.' The Dundee cake was the star of that occasion.

8 oz plain flour
¼ tsp salt
8 oz butter
6 oz caster sugar
4 large eggs
8 oz sultanas
8 oz currants
6 oz chopped mixed peel
3 oz glacé cherries
1 oz almonds
1 lemon
1 Tbs medium sherry
1 oz blanched almonds

Sieve flour with salt. □ Cream together butter and caster sugar until fluffy. □ Add eggs, one at a time, beating them well. □ Fold in sultanas, currants, chopped mixed peel, glacé cherries (quartered and rolled in flour), chopped almonds, and the grated rind of a lemon. □ Mix well. □ Add the lemon juice and medium sherry to get a stiff dropping consistency. □ Put into a well-buttered and greaseproof-lined 9in tin, decorate the top of the cake with almonds (split neatly in two) and bake in the centre of a moderate oven at 350 deg.F. (Gas Mark 4) for 1½ to 2 hours, or until a skewer pushed into the middle comes out dry.

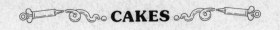

Selkirk Bannocks

I have my favourites among the plethora of Scottish heroes and heroines and, not unnaturally, food is connected with them. There are the obvious ones, such as Rob Roy and his grouse, but I like Black Agnes best. She was a raven-haired beauty who kept Castle Dunbar when her spouse, the Earl of March, was out ferreting the English. Insidiously, the enemy Earl of Salisbury crept up and tried to penetrate Agnes' keep, but she out-manoeuvred the noble lord, which fact has been made history in folk song. 'She kept astir in tower and trench/That brawling, boisterous Scottish Wench/Came I early, came I late/I found Black Agnes at the gate.' She was the bionic woman of the 14th century, and showed her contempt by dusting the battlements whenever the noble earl attacked. Her final insult, when both sides were starving, was to use the last of the castle's resources to send out to Salisbury a bottle of wine and a basket of bannocks.

4 oz unsalted butter
1 pt lukewarm milk
¾ oz fresh yeast
1 tsp brown sugar
Grating of nutmeg
2 lb plain flour
1 tsp salt
4 oz sultanas
2 oz candied peel
2 oz currants
4 oz caster sugar

119

Melt unsalted butter, but do not let it cook to oil. □ Add to it ½pt lukewarm milk. □ Cream fresh yeast with soft brown sugar and slowly mix it into the butter mixture. □ Sieve together plain flour and salt with nutmeg. □ Make a well and pour in the liquid to make a thick batter. □ Sprinkle the top with more flour and leave to work in a warm place as for bread. □ After 35 minutes it should be ready and then add as much of the lukewarm milk as is needed to make a soft dough. □ Knead well for 15 minutes and put back in a warm place to rise until it doubles its bulk. □ Now 'knock down' and knead in sultanas, chopped candied peel, currants, which have been slightly warmed, and caster sugar. □ Prove in a warm place for 30 minutes. □ Brush with milk and sugar mixed to make a glaze and bake at 450 deg.F. (Gas Mark 7) for 40 minutes. □ Serve in buttered slices.

Cherry Lemon Madeira Cake

Mother was an obsessive cook and when she dragged me around the opera circuit I became her taster-in-chief. The real crunch came when we toured Britain and Denmark in one year: both countries make more cakes than any others and such a diet can be very bad for a pubescent boy. I was soon

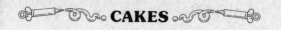

encouraged to take cookery lessons as something had to be done in the interest of self-preservation. This cake had its origins in farmland Essex. A plain Madeira is made the same way, except that you may omit the lemon and certainly the cherries.

6 oz unsalted butter
4 oz caster sugar
3 large eggs
1 lemon
8 oz self-raising flour
4 oz glacé cherries

Well butter an 8in cake tin which has a removable bottom. □ Cream unsalted butter and caster sugar together thoroughly (best done with a food mixer) then add one at a time large eggs, beating well after each additon. □ Now add the grated rind of lemon and its juice (do not worry if the mixture curdles at this stage, it will right itself with the addition of the flour). □ Fold in self-raising flour lightly. (Add a little milk if necessary, up to a maximum of 1 tablespoon). The mixture needs to be stiff to support the cherries — you have it right when it clings to the spoon but just drops when held high. □ Fold in quartered and floured cherries, keeping a few for the top of the cake. □ Turn into the prepared tin, dust the surface with caster sugar and position the remaining cherries. □ Bake at 350 deg.F. (Gas Mark 4) for approximately 1 hour. If you want to be sure the cake is cooked, test with a fine skewer — if it comes out clean as a whistle your cake is all right. □ Place a few whirls of lemon peel on the surface when set.

Orange Jumbles

One of my favourite picnics of recent years was thrown by me at Cove Hythe, a near-deserted beach in Suffolk. There amid remnants of Second World War sea defences I spread my snowy cloth and 200-year-old damask napkins (reluctantly, for all the other linen had been used up on luncheon and dinner parties the day before). For pudding I served apricot ice cream; but instead of serving the usual *langues-de-chat* to go with it I recalled a recipe from my beginnings. It is for orange jumbles, which go equally well with fruit salads.

4 oz unsalted butter
5 oz icing sugar
3 eggs
1 Tbs orange juice
1 tsp grated orange rind
4 oz plain flour

Cream well together unsalted butter and sifted icing sugar, then beat in unwhipped egg whites until absorbed. □ Now mix in vigorously orange juice, orange rind and plain flour. □ Butter a baking sheet and on it drop, well apart, spoonfuls of batter which should measure 1¼in across — they spread. □ Place in an oven preheated to 400 deg.F. (Gas Mark 6) and bake until edges turn golden — about 7-8 minutes. □ Remove the jumbles with a palette knife and curve around the handle of a wooden spoon. Makes 24-30 jumbles.

Bavarian Cherry Cake

Flattered, I never question photographers who want to take snaps of me; it must be something to do with my characterful face. For my cookery pieces I have been photographed as a Samurai by Clive Arrowsmith, Mr. Motto by Bob Brooks, montaged by Trevor Sutton as both lovers in a reconstruction of *Déjeuner sur l'herbe*, a racing driver by Tony Evans and a Canadian Mountie by John Perkins. But the photograph I like best was taken by Harri Peccinotti and is of a faintly mournful me, my lips dripping from a hearty bite into my cream-laden-home-cooked-Bavarian-Cherry-Cake. Now all this would be by the way, if I had not had several letters lately urging me to quote a chocolate cake recipe. So here is one for this, the best chocolate cake I know.

3 eggs
5 oz caster sugar
3 oz plain flour
⅓ oz cocoa powder
¼ pt single cream
½ pt double cream
16 oz can of morellos
2 tsp arrowroot
1 chocolate flake bar
Kirsch to taste

Grease with butter and line with greaseproof paper the base and sides of a 9in straight-sided sandwich tin, a separate sideband to come 1in over the edge. ☐ Make a sponge by whisking eggs in a large basin over a saucepan of hot water. ☐ Add caster sugar and whisk until a trail is left over the surface (takes 8-10 minutes). ☐ Fold in plain flour, sifted with cocoa powder. ☐ Turn into the baking tin and cook at 375 deg.F. (Gas Mark 5) for 30 minutes until well risen and firm to the touch. ☐ When completely cold, cut into three layers horizontally, and whip together single and double cream until soft peaks form. ☐ Stone the drained cherries — reserving 12 for decoration, and cut the remainder in half. ☐ Make the cherry juice up to ¼ pt with water, heat up the juice and add the hot juice to the arrowroot (previously creamed in a little cold juice). ☐ Bring to the boil to thicken and then cook for about 2 minutes until clear. ☐ Stir in the halved cherries and cool. ☐ Layer up the cake, using a third of the cream for the bottom layer and the cherries for the second layer, sprinkling each layer with a little kirsch. ☐ Completely mask the cake with the remaining cream and crumble chocolate over the centre. ☐ Arrange whole cherries around edge.

Aunty Hild's Fruit Loaf

I enjoy the letters I get: one was from Mrs. Kathleen Curry of Rostherne in Cheshire. She wrote, 'Aunty Hild lived in an old cottage in Cromford, Derbyshire. The front parlour opened on to the street and the kitchen was a draughty lean-to at the back, with an old brown shallow slopstone for the washing-up. Tea there was an unforgettable experience: scones, biscuits, melt-in-the-mouth sponge cakes — nothing was ever 'shop-bought'. When we go on holiday we always take Aunt Hild's Fruit Loaf. But last year I used another recipe, thinking it was one of yours. It was disastrous — solid and uninviting. Rather than tarnish my reputation as a capable cook, it went to the seagulls.' That recipe happily was not of my making. But I took Aunt Hild's recipe, tested it and declared it duly elected as the best I have ever tasted. Aunty Hild is well over 90 and is a resident of Lea Hurst. Here is her recipe, which kind Mrs Curry sent me.

5 oz unsalted butter
4 oz caster sugar
1 oz soft brown sugar
2 large eggs
8 oz self-raising flour
1 oz ground almonds
Pinch of salt
Grated rind of 1 lemon and 1 orange
5 oz mixed fruit
1 oz glacé cherries
Blanched almonds

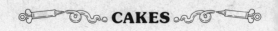
Soften unsalted butter in a bowl previously warmed in hot water and dried. □ Now beat into the butter caster sugar and soft brown sugar until the mixture is fluffy. (An electric food mixer does this best.) □ Then beat in eggs, one at a time. □ Fold in self-raising flour, ground almonds, salt and the grated rind of a lemon and an orange. □ Now fold in mixed fruit plus quartered glacé cherries (all previously dusted in a sieve with flour). □ Turn into a well-greased 8in by 5in loaf tin and dome the mixture. □ Stud with halved blanched almonds and bake at 350 deg.F. (Gas Mark 4) for 1¼ to 1½ hours or until a skewer comes out clean. □ It is superb warm and excellent when cold.

'Pics' from Wales

Mrs. Bevan lived in the corner house and was the organist in the chapel. A grand figure she made on a Sunday night when she would throw back her head (surmounted by a hat which would grace a bishop) and bring down her hands to strike a chord from the organ to lead the congregation into reprise after reprise of *Cwm Rhondda*. When everyone was in good voice the last verse would be sung five times. Mrs. Bevan was a widow-woman and her ten-shilling-a-week pension did not go far. She was not paid by the chapel, so she earned a little extra by making nettle pop and ginger beer to sell to us boys at a penny a flagon. She could sell all she produced since Dandelion and Burdock and even American Ice Cream Soda sold at tuppence a bottle in the shops. Even so, we should have still gone to her because there was always the chance of a bottle exploding, and that would bring forth from her a stream of Welsh not suitable for declaiming from the pulpit. I always tried to get there on baking days, for she made the best 'pics' in the valley: the formal name of this Welsh cake is *Pice ar y maen* and it was cooked on a solid iron bakestone balanced over an open fire between the oven top and brick placed on the hob which normally held the kettle.

1 lb plain flour
1 tsp baking powder
8 oz butter
Pinch of salt
6 oz caster sugar
6 oz currants
1 egg
Milk

Rub together flour, baking powder, butter and salt, as though making shortcrust pastry. ☐ Mix in caster sugar and currants (a mixture of currants and chopped stoned raisins can be used). ☐ Beat egg. ☐ Add to mixture, with a little milk, to make a smooth paste. ☐ Roll out to ¼in thickness and cut into 3 in rounds. ☐ Cook on a bakestone, skillet or griddle (alternatively use a lightly greased, heavy frying pan over a moderate heat) for about 3 minutes each side. ☐ Best served warm, but can be served cold.